SOCIAL HUMANISM

Interfaith Treasures Uncovered

Under this Series, the Publishers endeavor to focus on Comparative Studies pertaining to Christian Faith & Living in the central matrix and Hinduism, Buddhism, Sikhism, Islam, Judaism, etc., on the peripheral. The Studies shall cover topics like Literature & Poetry, Indigenous Philosophizing, Ethical response towards Agriculture, Health & Healing, Science & Technology, Ecofeminist Theology, Sociological approach towards Human Rights, Law & Politics, Arts, History of Ideas, Ancient Civilizations, Cultural Contiguity, Religious Cosmologies & Mysticism, Footsteps of famous Theologians, World Peace & Harmony, Global Capitalism, Network Marketing, Cybertheology, Population & Demographics, Epigraphic Studies, Contextualized Education, and many others. We welcome a Mss. on any topic/s mentioned, whether they are original works, scholarly monographs, collections of conference papers, revised dissertations, or translations of historical documents. Through the Series, we are striving to put forward published works that may help Institutions, Academic Bodies, Researchers, Scholars and the World at large in furthering their respective knowledge and understanding on the concerned subject. We welcome your comments on our efforts and further suggestions on how we can foster the upcoming books on parallel interfaces between and among Christianity and other religions.

Interfaith Treasures Uncovered - 15

SOCIAL HUMANISM

Dr. Ambedkar's Social Philosophy in reference to the Dalit Christians

Robert Pen

Christian World Imprints™

First Published in 2018 by

Christian World Imprints(TM)
Christian Publishing & Books from India
H-12 Bali Nagar, **New Delhi-110015**
info@christianworldimprints.com
www.ChristianWorldImprints.com
Phone: +91 11 25465925

ISBN: 978-93-5148-301-4

Printed in India.

Contents

Preface

Human beings are social beings. They therefore need to live in harmony with those around them and it is only there that they can grow up and mature as human beings. Human beings cannot hope to ride the world until and unless they have created for each member of the human race, basic rights of freedom and equality which will allow them for full development and unrestricted use of human intelligence and capabilities. Occasionally, a human being has been made to suffer at the hands of other human beings driven mad by power – religious, political, economic or social. In such a situation the conscience of humanity has been outraged, and the cry has gone round for some sort of guarantees to afford protection to one human being against the tyranny of his fellow human beings, so that they can be assured of at least their rights to life, liberty and security of person.

A similar situation was present in Ambedkar's time when the backward class people of those days, namely the Shudras and the Untouchables, were made to suffer at the hands of Caste Hindus. Ambedkar's social philosophy was in response to their struggle for liberation. He could not tolerate the unjust environment – social, economic, political and religious – which had been holding humanity in fetters for centuries. During his revolt, he developed a sort of socio-humanistic philosophy which, in a sporadic manner continued to grow till the last days of his life. He stands for human dignity and freedom, for simplicity, integrity, liberty, equality, social and economic justice. He is opposed to any social order or institution or any creed or practice which involves injustice, violence and suppression of human personality. He therefore exposes the evil traditions and blind beliefs of the Caste-ridden Hindu social order. This book is an attempt to understand these various insights of Ambedkar on 'Social Humanism' and his valuable contribution towards the creation of a new social order.

The most beautiful thing that has happened to me while working on this book has been the emergence of a constant urge within myself, to arrive at a humanistic vision of reality. I have been made to realize in the course of this book that it is in creating a humanistic vision that we live in the whole of reality, and that only a humanistic vision of reality can bring harmony into our social living. I found this quest being fulfilled to a great extent in the socio-humanistic insight of Ambedkar into reality. Moreover, I feel that Ambedkar has ignited within me the unquenchable fire of a passion for humanistic wholeness. I hope to keep it burning for the whole of my life. This book has turned out for me to be more a personal vision of life than a purely academic achievement. With this brief account of my philosophical itinerary in this book I usher in the exposition of Ambedkar's insights on 'Social Humanism'.

Chapter 1

Introduction

The social philosophy of Ambedkar, according to me, is very much relevant to our times. I have therefore undertaken the study of his social philosophy with the focus on his insight on 'Social Humanism'.

In the present chapter my concern is to examine the present social situation so as to understand the full implications of his social philosophy. I will conclude with a brief note on his socio-religious background.

1. The Relevance of Ambedkar's Social Philosophy Today

Society in India is based on an unique form of social order known as the 'Caste system'. Indian society is divided horizontally and vertically into thousands of Castes. The Castes are further divided into sub-Castes or sub-sub Castes. People belonging to these different Castes follow their rules and customs minutely. Each Caste member keeps himself at a certain distance from the person belonging to some other Caste. The practice of such an attitude has been continued for centuries. In recent years, this problem of 'the observance of Castes' has become acute. The lowest Caste people have become very sensitive towards the issue of ill-treatment and oppression that they face at the hands of the upper Caste people. The exposure to various educational facilities and mass-media has brought them to a kind of self-awareness leading them to fight for their human rights. Various Dalit movements are working efficiently to annihilate the social evil of the Caste system and to acquire social justice for themselves.

In this respect, the example of Ambedkar is noteworthy, as he dedicated his whole life for the eradication of the most heinous disease in the Hindu society, namely the Untouchability. Being an Untouchable by birth helped him to reach the depth of the problems faced by the Dalit brethren. As the leader and champion of the depressed classes, he inspired millions of his followers to break away the age-old shackles in order to create a new society. With all vehemence, he denounced the Caste system and the Brahmanical writings which supported this inhuman institution for centuries together. He is hailed as a prophet by the Dalits today for his enriching contribution towards their cause which is very much relevant to our times.

As a Christian, I am conscious of the discrimination against our Dalit brethren within the Catholic Church. It is ironic that Christianity whose unique attraction was equality should thrust discrimination at its lower orders. Dalit Christians, being aware of their indignities due to Casteism, are now rebelling against the social injustice that has kept them out of educational institutes, adequate representation in clergy, community leadership, etc. Due to such a social situation, they too have been attracted towards Ambedkar's 'Social Humanism' which gives them a ray of hope for their social upliftment within the Church.

To understand the relevance of Ambedkar's social philosophy fully, I have taken a closer look at the dimension of 'Casteism' in India today.

1.1. The Casteism in India

Although, it has been nearly seventy years since India became independent, the struggle of the SC/ST/BCs for equality and justice against the upper Caste people still exists. In the villages, the high Caste Hindu people still address the low Caste people not by their name but by their Caste names. Today, the localities are divided and demarcated not on the basis of the property that they hold but on the basis of their Caste. The slums are reserved exclusively for the Dalits. The Untouchables in the villages still live on the outskirts of the village. Thus, the 'Castes' are being minutely followed in the villages as well as in the cities.

We see tremendous controversies in the country over the Caste issue. The people, the masses, know who belongs to which Caste. It has become an essential part of the general knowledge in India. A landlord wants to find out his tenant's Caste before renting his house. Today, the political parties including the Marxist give party tickets for election only on the basis of the Caste of the candidate. In short, everything is decided on the basis of Caste and everybody knows about it in India. There is no secrecy about it, for even the newspapers report this boldly.

A Caste-wise census of the ministers, judges, ambassadors, vise chancellors, secretaries to government, heads of industrial enterprises and banks shows that Brahmins are occupying over 70% of these positions, while the most degrading profession of scavenging, sweeping is still reserved for the Untouchables. Over 40% of the landless agricultural labourers in the country are the Untouchable and the Tribals. We never find a Brahmin living in a slum while it appears as though the slums are reserved for Dalits.[1]

The Indian communist say Untouchability, Caste, superstition and oppression of women will all vanish the moment the society gets industrialized and the exploited become economically strong. Our experience has belied these hopes. Caste system continues to exist even when Dalits and Hindus both get educated. Many Dalit doctors posted in the rural areas do not get houses because of their Caste, although educationally they are much higher than the Hindus. We have hundreds of such cases of Caste discrimination even against educated Untouchables. Even judges, IAS and IPS officers are complaining of discrimination by their Hindu colleagues. Our experience in India has proved that cities are more Caste conscious

---

[1] V.T. Rajshekar, *The Dilemma of Class and Caste in India* (Bangalore: Dalit Sahitya Academy, 1984), 16.

than the villages. In fact, the more educated a person is the more bigoted he becomes. Today all those who talk about Caste, shout about Caste, and protest against Caste are all 'educated people.'[2]

It appears as though the Dalits were born to serve the upper Caste. As long as they are docile, obedient, work as slaves of Hindus they are tolerated. The moment they express even slight resentment, let alone protest, they are kicked, killed and burnt. This is what happened at Chunder in Andhra Pradesh on August 6, 1991, where over twenty-five Untouchables were massacred by the ruling Reddys. "Hundreds of Hindus in a well-laid-out conspiracy chased the unnamed Untouchable men through paddy fields, caught them, hacked them to pieces, dumped them into gunny bags and footballed them into the canal at different places so that the flooded canal carried the bags into the nearby Bay of Bengal. And in this conspiracy the Hindu police collaborated."[3]

In another incident at Chilakurti of Nalgonda District on August 14, 1991 three Reddys disrobed a twenty-five year old woman, forced a quarter litre of arrack down her throat and paraded her naked on the streets, her hands tied behind with her blouse. This woman, Verapidatha Muthamma, who belonged to the backward 'Golla' Caste (shepherd), is a servant in the house and farm of one of the assailants. Not satisfied with this gruesome atrocity, they kept her for public view for an hour at 'Santha' (weekly market) at Chilakurti.[4]

On November 7, 2012 more than 200 houses were burnt in the Dharmapuri district of Tamil Nadu. The violence started after an "upper-Caste" Vanniyar girl from Sellankottai village eloped with a Dalit boy from a neighbouring colony. A panchayat meeting had ruled that the girl must return to her family. When she refused to return to her family, such was the insult to the father of the girl that he committed suicide by hanging himself. When his body was discovered, an enraged mob of over 1,500 rampaged through the

---

[2] V.T. Rajshekar, *The Dilemma of Class and Caste in India,* 15-18.

[3] V.T. Rajshekar, "Chundur proves non-Hindu Dalit can't live with Hindus: separate electorate and settlement as solution", *Dalit Voice,* Vol. 10, September 1-15, 1991, 3.

[4] V.T. Rakshekar, "Reddys strip BC woman", *Dalit Voice,* Vol. 10, September 16-31, 1991, 11.

nearby Dalit settlements burning more than 200 houses and allegedly looting valuables worth lakhs. More than 90 men were arrested later and over 1000 policemen had to be deployed to bring back normalcy in the area.[5]

In 2014, three were murdered and their mutilated body parts were strewn about on a farm in Ahmednagar, Maharashtra. The three victims were members of a Dalit family: Sanjay Jadhav, his wife Jayashree and their teenage son Sunil. The crime happened in the middle of the night on the 21st of October in the quiet village of Javkhede Khalasa. It later came to light that the killings were quite possibly "honour killings" because of an illicit affair between a member of the Jadhav family and an "upper-Caste" married woman who lived close to the farm.[6]

The above examples are just a few of the innumerable atrocities that are taking place every year in our country. The Dalits thus are given inhuman treatment at the hands of upper Caste Hindus. They are quite helpless without the help of various government facilities and organization controlled by the upper Caste Hindus. Unable to fight back against the injustice done to them, they are forced to accept their servile condition and oppression under the upper Caste people. Although, the democracy of our country stresses equal participation of all groups, the Hindu ethos does not allow it. Hence, such incidences of violence take place when the Dalits demand participation and equal sharing. This proves that today in our country the Dalits are not able to live together in peace with their Hindu brethren.

The Dalits today have become the most degraded, downtrodden, exploited and the least educated in India. They are not able to create a revolution to fight for their rights because among themselves there is a lack of unity. The Caste system has not only divided these Dalits from the upper classes but also within themselves they do not have sufficient unity to come together and fight for their common

[5] Bodhisattwa Debnath, "Caste Discrimination in India: 10 Cases You Wish Did Not Happen" May 19, 2016, 3. https://blog.timetoswipe.com/Caste-discrimination-india-10-cases-you-wish-did-not-happen/ Accessed on 8/4/2018.

[6] Debnath, "Caste Discrimination in India: 10 Cases You Wish Did Not Happen" May 19, 2016, 5.

cause. "Today the Dalits in India are kicked, killed, burnt, raped and their property destroyed. Is it because they are poor? If they are poor why are the other poor Hindus not subjected to similar treatment? Are the Dalits the only poor people of India? Dalits 'including tribals' constitute about 30% of the Indian population. But the government of India figures say over 50% of the population is living below poverty line."[7] Although, these people are poor like the Dalits, they are not attacked. This goes to show that poverty is not the reason for the attacks on Dalits. It is their Untouchability – socially, culturally, religiously different from others – which is the main cause of their dehumanization. This Untouchability is nothing else but the inhuman treatment of the upper Caste people towards the lower Caste people. In short, ultimately it is the 'Caste difference' that matters.

IDSN (International Dalit Solidarity Network) which is working globally against Caste based discrimination point out that Caste discrimination is a highly politicized and sensitive issue in India. Despite constitutional safeguards and special legislation for the protection of the country's 201 million 'Scheduled Castes' (the official term for Hindu, Sikh and Buddhist Dalits), violations of their fundamental human rights continue on a massive scale. Key issues include access to justice and rising violence against Dalits, multiple discriminations against Dalit women, slavery and child labour, discrimination in education, Untouchability and access to basic services, including humanitarian aid, social and economic rights and shrinking space for Dalit human rights defenders.[8]

Within the scope of this book the concept of 'Casteism' needs to be examined further on two different planes, namely, the national dimension of Caste and the Christian dimension of Caste.

---

[7] V.T. Rajshekar, *The Dilemma of Class and Caste in India,* 11.

[8] "Caste discrimination in India", IDSN Briefing Note–India 2016, 1. http://idsn.org/wp-content/uploads/2016/09/IDSN-briefing-note-India-2016.pdf Accessed on 8/4/2018.

1.2. The National Dimension of Caste (Reservation v/s 'Merit and Efficiency')

Another major burning issue for which the SC/ST/BCs (scheduled Caste/scheduled tribe/backward class) in our country today are fighting so dearly is that of reservation. The country today is ruled by the upper Caste 'merit and efficiency' reducing and breaking the country to pieces. In V. T. Rajshekar's words, "What we have in India today is upper Caste colonialism if not brahmanical tyranny."[9]

The Dalits today have been crushed by this 'merit and efficiency'. It prevents them from getting better jobs, socio-economic facilities and thus rising to the level of the upper Caste people. For the upper Caste people 'merit' means efficiency and reservations means 'inefficiency'. That is why they raise the question of merit and efficiency whenever reservations to SC/ST/BCs and other minorities is mentioned but "there is no statistical basis or expert evidence to support the assumption that efficiency will be impaired if reservation is continued or if reservation exceeds a certain percentage or even if reservation is extended to promotional posts."[10]

Although, the reservation policy is meant to give equal human rights to all the sections of the society in proportion to their population, still many people, mainly the upper Castes, are fighting against it. The reaction against reservation is based on two considerations: "First, it hurts a person's sense of fair play to see that a more 'meritorious' candidate has been left out in preference to less 'meritorious' person on purely extraneous grounds. Secondly, it is argued, that by selecting candidates with lower 'merit' against reserved quota vacancies, the nation is being deprived of the services of the best talent that is available to it."[11] This sort of argument suffers from as serious fallacy regarding the nature of 'merit'. The student coming from the fairly well off middle-class family is well guided in his studies by his educated parents and teachers; he has been to a good school providing a wide range of extra-curricular activities. The society in which he lives makes him fully aware of the nature of the

---

[9] V.T. Rajshekar, *The Dilemma of Class and Caste in India,* 28.

[10] V.T. Rajshekar, *The Dilemma of Class and Caste in India,* 31.

[11] V.T. Rajshekar, *The Dilemma of Class and Caste in India,* 32.

highly competitive world. At home, he has all the facilities available to him. The student coming from the backward class is deprived of all these luxuries owing to his rural background. Assuming that both these students had the same level of intelligence at the time of their birth, it is obvious that owing to the vast difference in social, cultural and environmental factors the former will beat the latter by length in any competitive field.[12] Is it not unfair then to judge both of them by the same yardstick? Can we speak of 'merit' or 'equality' between these 'two unequals'? Is it not right for the SC/ST/BCs and the other minorities to fight for reservations which are the guarantee of their 'human rights'?

In this regard, the Mandal Commission Report which favors the reservations for the BC people has been strongly put down by the Brahmins and the upper Caste people. Their main objection is that the Mandal report has taken 'Caste' as the sole criterion. In the eyes of the critics the Mandal has 'over-emphasized Caste'; it is because the BCs happened to be the least educated and the poorest.[13]

According to V.T. Rajshekar, who was closely associated with the preparation of the 'Mandal Commission Report', the report is prepared scientifically taking into consideration the present situation of our country. In preparation of the report, he says, the Mandal had adopted three different yardsticks: social, education and economic. Further he comments, that it is acceptable to over 85% of the country's 850 million population, which includes 65% population of SC/ST/BCs and the 20% religious minorities. Still the remaining 15% upper Caste population, through their anti-Mandal campaigns, agitations and violence, has managed to stop the implementation of this report in the society.[14]

From the above account it appears that all the efforts of the upper Caste people are geared towards preservation of Caste which brings them so much pleasure, power, position, and privileges without

---

[12] V.T. Rajshekar, *The Dilemma of Class and Caste in India,* 32-33.

[13] V.T. Rajshekar, "Reservations meant to elevate, empower a group but not an individual", *Dalit Voice,* Vol. 11, December 16-31, 1991, 20.

[14] V.T. Rajshekar, "Reservations meant to elevate, empower a group but not an individual", 19-20.

doing any work.[15] Thus, the problem of reservation is in reality a problem between the higher Caste people, who are struggling to preserve the Caste differences and Dalits, who are fighting for their human rights and social status in the society.

1.3. The Christian Dimension of Caste

Let us begin with the very basic question – why has the Christian population not gone beyond 3% in the past several centuries since Christianity came to India? Though there is a harvest field among the Untouchables and Tribals, the Church has not been able to convert the high Caste Hindus. Why?

Most of the converts to Christianity in India today belong to the Untouchables and tribal communities. Those belonging to a higher Caste are not interested in quitting Hinduism because, though poor, they are not oppressed. The lower Caste people are disgusted with Hinduism because Caste division has the divine sanction, a theological foundation in Hinduism. These converts, who embraced Christianity to get out of the suffocating gas chamber of Hinduism, are once again discriminated within the Church.

Rev. Azariah says: "Over a million Hindu converts to Christianity, members of the Roman Catholic Church, are more or less ruled by Caste. The protestant missionaries likewise found it difficult in early days to overcome Caste prejudice among their converts and not many years ago in the Madras Presidency, clergymen were compelled to use different cups for each separate Caste, when they celebrated the 'Lord's Supper.'"[16] He further laments: "I have recently learnt with deep pain and shock that specifically in four out of twenty-one dioceses, two in Kerala and two in Tamil Nadu, separate worshipping centers of churches are being used for separate congregations in the same locality within the distance of a furlong or two."[17] The above example clearly shows that the attitude of Caste divisions among

---

[15] V.T. Rajshekar, "Reservations meant to elevate, empower a group but not an individual", 21.

[16] M. Azariah, *The Un-Christian side of the Indian Church* (Bangalore: Dalit Sahitya Academy, 1989), 9.

[17] M. Azariah, *The Un-Christian side of the Indian Church*, 10.

Christians is not very much different from those of the orthodox Hindus.

Today in India nearly 75% of Christians are from the Untouchable community. Yet most of the bishops, priests, sisters are from the 'upper Caste Christians'. A large number of institutions, colleges, the high posts such as vicar general, procurator, director of social works and pastoral centers, rectors of minor and major seminaries are often in the hands of eight million upper Caste (Hindu) converts to Christianity.[18] The SC Christians of today have been twice alienated. First, by the mere fact of their conversion they have been disowned by their other community members and are denied the constitutionally provided privileges and compensatory benefits available to other 'Scheduled Caste'; i.e., they become non eligible to the social handicap benefits in the form of reservations and concessions for employment and educational opportunities and for reserved seats in the legislature. Secondly, within the Church where they hope to get their rights, self-respect and equal treatment like other fellow Christians, they continue to be discriminated against. "The problem with the SC Christians is not only that they are discriminated against and looked down upon by their own fellow Christians but they themselves have accepted their subordinate and servile status in society, even within the Church society."[19]

Thus, according to V.T. Rajshekar, the Christian Dalit suffers from a five-fold alienation and oppression:

1. The non-converted Dalits look upon them with suspicion when the Christian Dalits seek government assistance as they are considered already uplifted by missionary patronage.
2. Upper Caste Christians treat Christian Dalits contemptuously.
3. Discrimination by the Christian hierarchy.
4. Upper Caste Hindus show discrimination to Dalit Christians.
5. The state is against reservation to Dalit Christians.[20]

---

[18] M. Azariah, *The Un-Christian side of the Indian Church*, 10.

[19] M. Azariah, *The Un-Christian side of the Indian Church*, 10-11.

[20] Father Shouri, "Dalit Christians' threat to walk out of 'Hindu' Church", *Dalit Voice,* Vol. 10, August 16-31, 1991, 16.

The purpose of conversion therefore remains a question in everybody's mind. Is conversion taking place merely to increase the strength of the Christian community so that they can very well stand against other religious communities in India? Is it because the missionaries pity the condition of these SC/ST/BC people? Is it done by the missionaries for the sole purpose of their self glorification or is it done for the sake of pleasing the people in authority of the Church today? Or is it done to spread the message of equality, brotherhood and love given to them by Jesus Christ? If so, why are these converts treated the same way as they were treated before? Why is it that there is not much change in the social condition of these converts?

Besides the plight of the Christian converts there are various other serious issues which are troubling the SC/ST/BCs today, such as the struggle against inequality, the present class-Caste dilemma, their quest for cultural identity, etc. The struggle of SC/ST/BCs today needs to be analyzed and studied in depth. Before searching for the answers to all their problems one needs to understand their background. There is no better person than Dr. Ambedkar who has studied all these problems so deeply. Being one of them he has been successful enough to analyze their problems systematically, methodically and scientifically. His efforts and contribution for the upliftment of these people are of great value today. It is with these thoughts in mind that I have undertaken the study of 'The Social Philosophy of Dr. Ambedkar'.

2. The Socio-religious Background of Dr. Ambedkar

Every thinker philosophizes within a context and a background. Their philosophical thinking is very much influenced by the prevalent traditions of their time and the social-cultural environment around them. To have an authentic understanding of their thoughts it is necessary for us to place ourselves within their socio-cultural background. This will enable us to understand the mind and the thinking process of that particular philosopher to a certain extent. In our present endeavor this calls for the study of socio-religious background of Ambedkar which has helped him develop his social philosophy.

Dr. Ambedkar is primarily known as a leader of the Untouchables. He dedicated his whole life for the cause of the Untouchables. In fact it became his life's mission. A man of his caliber, so intellectual and brilliant, could have easily climbed the towers of any other field of life. What was it that made him take up this task of Untouchability? To have a better understanding of his work and mission, let us have a look at the socio-religious background in which he was born and brought up. This includes the understanding of inhuman social conditions of the servile classes - the Shudras and the Untouchable – prevalent at that time.

Before the birth of Ambedkar, the Shudras and the Untouchables would receive sub-human treatment at the hands of upper Caste Hindus. Their life was full of poverty and injustice, illiteracy and exploitation, tyranny and oppression. This artificial social behavior-pattern of Hindu society did not go unchallenged. From time to time many great personalities like Eknath, Tukaram, etc., launched a protest against the existing social system to free it from all social evil. In spite of all their efforts the condition of the servile class – the Shudras and the Untouchables – continued to deteriorate. Dhananjay Keer explains it in the following words:

> Their social disabilities were specific and severe and numerous. Their touch, shadow and even voice were deemed by the Caste Hindus to be polluting. So they had to clear the way at the approach of a Caste Hindu. They were forbidden to keep certain domestic animals, to use certain metals for ornaments; were obliged to wear a particular type of footwear, and were forced to occupy the dirty, dingy and unhygienic outskirts of villages and towns for habitation where they lived in dark, insanitary and miserable smoky shanties or cottages.[21]

Despite the great effort made by the great saints and other reform movements, the Shudras and the Untouchables were denied the use of public wells, and were condemned to drink any filthy

---

[21] Dhananjay Keer, *Dr. Ambedkar: Life and Mission* (Bombay: Popular Prakashan, 1954), 1.

water they could find. They were even denied of their basic rights of education, equality and liberty. Being born in an Untouchable family, Ambedkar too lived the life of his community people who were struggling to keep themselves alive under inhuman conditions. He himself suffered terribly at the hands of social evils of Caste and Untouchability.[22]

Ambedkar was born on April 14, 1891 at Khow in an Untouchable Mahar family, whose forefathers were treated for more than two thousand years as worse than dogs, whose touch was regarded as pollution and whose shadow a sacrilege. His early schooling was desultory. He was often not permitted to sit along with his classmates; he was barred from studying Sanskrit lest he pollute the 'holy' language; he was denied water even to quench his thirst. He had to face all these and a legion of such inhuman barbarities simply because by accident of birth he was an Untouchable.[23]

The innate courage and an unshakeable determination led him not only to pass the matriculation examination in 1907 but also to secure a scholarship in 1913 from Maharaja of Baroda for higher studies in U.S.A, through the help of a well-known social reformer Sri Krishnaji Keluskar. At Columbia University in New York, Ambedkar became a favorite student of the famous economist Dr. Seligman. He wrote brilliantly on Indian problems and in June 1916 Columbia University accepted his thesis 'National Divident of India' for the degree of Ph.D. He returned to India as a learned man in 1917 and was appointed military secretary to Maharaja of Baroda.[24]

To his great disappointment Ambedkar found that his education and high office could not wash away the stigma of Untouchability. He was treated as a social leper by Caste Hindus. Although, he was the chief in the office, his Hindu subordinates would not touch his desk. Even peons hurled papers at him. He could not get a house to live in. With great difficulty he acquired a place in a Parsee inn, but even this was not tolerated by Caste Hindus who forced the Parsee proprietor of the inn to eject the tenant. Ambedkar had to leave the city in utter

---

[22] Keer, *Dr. Ambedkar: Life and Mission*, 1-2.

[23] Keer, *Dr. Ambedkar: Life and Mission*, 9.

[24] Keer, *Dr. Ambedkar: Life and Mission*, 19-32.

disgust. These cruel cuts filled him with bitterness towards the upper Caste Hindus which never cooled down completely.[25]

In November 1918, Ambedkar went from Baroda to Bombay and became professor of Economics at the Sydenham College of Commerce. However, he felt that if he wanted to devote his enormous resource of energy and brains to the removal of Untouchability then there was no alternative for him but to earn his living independently. So, he decided to take up a career in law. Therefore, in July 1920 he left for London where he was awarded the degree of D.Sc. in Economics. He also studied at Bonn University in Germany for a few months. He returned to India in 1923 and started practicing in Bombay High Court. He soon became famous as an able Barrister. At the same time, he worked hard for the upliftment of the Untouchables. Within a few years he became the best known Untouchable leader and in 1927 the Government nominated him to Bombay Legislative Council. In October 1928, he was invited to give evidence before Simon Commission. On September 6, 1930, he was invited by the viceroy to attend the Round Table Conference (R.T.C.) as the spokesperson of the depressed classes. By his great learning, forceful oratory, unbending will power and phenomenal energy, Ambedkar made a great impact at R.T.C. He then came to be recognized as the chief spokesman of Untouchables. He showed great statesmanship and entered into Poona Pact with upper Caste Hindu leaders, which on the one hand saved the life of Mahatma Gandhi and on the other hand gave better terms to the depressed classes.[26]

During the Second World War, Ambedkar rose to new eminence. In July 1941, he was appointed on the Defence Advisory Committee. A year later he was appointed Labour Member of the Executive council of the viceroy, and thus attained the highest post to which an Indian could have been appointed in those days. Yet the crowning achievement of Ambedkar's life was still to come. In August 1947, he became the first Law Minister of free India.

[25] Keer, *Dr. Ambedkar: Life and Mission*, 33-34.

[26] Keer, *Dr. Ambedkar: Life and Mission*, 39-45.

Further on August 29, 1947, the constituent Assembly appointed a Drafting committee with Ambedkar as its chairman.[27]

Thus an Untouchable who was chased out from hotels, hostels, saloons and temples as a despicable Mahar, became the chief architect of the constitution of his motherland and was hailed as 'Modern Manu.'[28] The very social environment in which he lived, suffered, experienced humiliation from the Caste Hindus, led him to develop within himself the urge to fight for human dignity, liberty and equality – in short, for Social Humanism.

---

[27] Keer, *Dr. Ambedkar: Life and Mission*, 338-392.

[28] Keer, *Dr. Ambedkar: Life and Mission*, 394.

Chapter 2

Traditional Hindu Social Order

In the previous chapter I have tried to show the relevance of Ambedkar's social humanism in the present 'Caste-ridden' society. A brief sketch of his socio-religious background too was drawn in this respect. The task of this chapter is to study the salient features of traditional Hindu Social Order, namely the Varna and the Caste system, which are highlighted and criticized by Ambedkar in his social philosophy. My main concern is, therefore, to examine the evolution process of Varnas and Castes, and to study briefly the features of the Caste system.

1. The Evolution of Varnas and Castes

Every society is bound to have some sort of 'social classification'. It depends upon the differences in man's natural endowment, intelligence, special abilities and talents, personality traits and innate characteristics. Social stratification is a phenomenon which would be impossible to abolish in any society. The Indian society, in this respect, is marked by the classification on the basis of Varnas and Jatis (Castes), as they are the most important governing principles of the Hindu social organization. It is a peculiar characteristic of Indian society as against the 'class' based social stratification in other societies. While reflecting upon the problem of Caste and Untouchability from Ambedkar's perspective, it is necessary for us to understand the evolution of the four Varnas and nearly 3000 Jatis of the present day.

1.1. The Varna System

It must be mentioned at the outset that all the literary accounts of the important aspects of Caste centre around the four orders in society, namely, Brahmins, Kshatriyas, Vaishyas and Shudras, and not the multifarious groups which are the present-day Castes. These four classes of the Hindu society were regularly treated as Varnas in Vedas and the later literature such as Upanishads, so much so, that popularly the Hindu religion came to be defined as Varnasrama Dharma. Although, the word 'Varna' literally means 'colour', there are various theories as regards the origin of these Varnas. Each one of them needs to be explained further.

i) The Guna Theory:

The guna theory holds that each individual, a form of Prakrti (nature), is made up of the three gunas: 'sattva', 'rajas' and 'tamas'. There is a constant movement inherent in these elements. Each has a tendency to gain supremacy over the other. It is this inherent movement that leads to the infinite permutations and combinations of the gunas, and, then to the manifold variety of the human being and its nature.[29] Further, according to this theory, there are four Varnas corresponding to these three gunas. Those in whom the sattvic guna gained supremacy over the other two gunas were the Brahmins; the rajasic guna was prominent among the Kshatriyas and the Vaishyas while the Shudras were the tamasic people.

ii) Occupational Theory:

The word Varna is derived from the Sanskrit word 'vri' meaning 'to choose'. Varna therefore was defined as to choose one's occupation

[29] D.R. Jatava, *The Social Philosophy of B.R. Ambedkar* (Agra: Phoenix Publication House, 1962), 74.

according to one's gunas (innate qualities) and karma. It is found that in the Vedic times there were no restrictions as regards particular occupations for a person belonging to a particular Varna. Thus, a person born as a Brahmin could take the occupation of a physician without thereby in any way degrading his social status. In fact there is no trace of heredity defining the occupation of an individual in early literature.[30]

iii) The Racial Theory:

The Shudras of the Rigvedic period seem to be no other than the non-Aryans, the Dasas or the Dasyus who differed from the fair-skinned Aryans on account of their dark complexion, flat nose, unintelligibility of speech, absence of sacrificing and worship of God, prevalence of foreign customs – all of which were obviously strange to the Aryans. They were kept by the Aryans as slaves. There is no obvious explanation of the term Shudra which later came to signify the Dasas. It is, however, suggested that 'Shudra' was probably the name of some prominent Dasa tribe, and, in course of time, the word became synonymous with the whole community of slaves, by usage.[31]

iv) The Origin of Varnas as given in the Hindu Shastras:

a) Rig Veda: In the Rig Veda only three classes of society are frequently mentioned, and named: Brahma, Kshatra, and Vis. The first two represented broadly the two professions of the poet-priest and the warrior-chief, while the third division was a group comprising of all the common people. It is only in one of the later hymns, the Purusha Sukta that a reference has been made to four orders of society as emanating from the sacrifice of the Primeval Being. They are named as Brahmans, Rajanya, Vaishya, and Shudra, who are said to have come from the mouth, the arms, the thighs, and the feet of the creator. The particular limbs associated with these divisions and the order in which they are mentioned probably indicate their status

[30] Pandharinath J. Prabhu, *Hindu Social Organization* (Bombay: Popualr Prakashan, 1961), 287.

[31] Prabhu, *Hindu Social Organization*, 287.

in the society of the time, though no such interpretation is directly given in the hymn.[32]

There is a reference contained in the Rig Veda (c.1200-900 B.C.), which suggests a second theory of Varna origins, namely that the system was formed within a group of families claiming common descent from Brahma, the mythical forefather. Initially the father was the Brahmin, the priest and teacher, the brother the warrior and protector, the sister the keeper of the household, and so on. However, after a few generations such organization became impossible to perpetuate so groups of individuals with the same roles drew apart into separate guilds or Castes.[33]

The origin of the four classes (the Chaturvarnya theory) is repeated in most of the later works, such as Taittiriya Samhita, Satpatha Brahmana, etc., with slight variations and interpretative additions. Taittiriya Samhita stresses that deities were created simultaneously with the creation of the first three classes while no deities were created along with Shudra. Hence, they are disqualified for sacrifice.[34]

b) Upanishads: The Brihadaranyaka Upanishad gives us an account of the origin of the Varnas in the following way: In the beginning there was only Brahman; alone, he could not prosper well. Therefore, he further created a form (or a pattern/type) with a view to welfare, viz. the Kshatra. This consisted of the gods like Indra, Varuna, Soma, Rudra, Parjanya, Yama, Mritya and Isana. Still, however, Brahman found that it could not fare satisfactorily; therefore it created the Vaishya-hood in the form of the gods like Vasus, Rudras, Adityas, Visye-devas and the Maruts. Even then, Brahman could not make good progress; so it created Shudra Varna in the form of the god Pushan. In spite of these creations, again, Brahman did not develop well; therefore, he still further created the form of Dharma for welfare (of Brahman, or of human beings). The earthly Varnas are in the opinions of Brihadaranyaka Upanishad thus

[32] G.S. Ghurye, *Caste and Class in India* (Bombay: The Popular Book Depot, 1950), 50.

[33] Sophie Baker, *Caste* (Calcutta: Rupa and Co, 1991), 44.

[34] G.S. Ghurye, *Caste and Class in India*, 45-46.

created out of these divine Varnas. This theory does not refer to any social gradation amongst the Varnas. On the contrary, each Varna was conceived as created with a view to contributing to the social welfare.[35]

c) Bhagavad Gita: Another theory of Varna origin can be attributed to a reference in the Bhagavad Gita (ch. iv,v. 13) to the words of Brahma: "The four Castes were created by Me according to differences in aptitudes and action of Men. Though I am its creator, know Me to be incapable of action or change". Philosophers studying this work believe that the reasoning behind Caste has an emphasis on guna (aptitude) and karma (function) but not Jati (birth and sub-Caste). The design of the embryonic Caste system was thus on man's inherent nature - each and every one of us possesses three main characteristics: pure qualities (meditative and contemplative), active qualities (the need to work and desire to participate and contribute) and qualities of inertia and lethargy (a lack of both willingness to utilize the mind and intellectual conceptions). Social position, Jati, is then dictated by these characteristics.[36]

d) Mahabharata: In Mahabharata while explaining the origin of the Varnas to Bharadwaja Bhrigu rishi says that at first the whole world consisted of Brahmanas. Although, they were created equally by Brahman, on account of their act, they have been divided into various Varnas. The theory goes on to explain how the four Varnas and other Castes arose out of the one original class of Dvijas (twice-born). Those who found excessive pleasure in enjoyment became possessed with these attributes of harshness and anger: endowed with courage, and unmindful of their own dharma, those Dvijas, possessing the qualities of redness, became Kshatriyas. Those again, who, unmindful of the duties laid down for them, were endowed with both the qualities of redness and darkness and followed the occupation of cattle-breeding and agriculture, became Vaishyas. Those Dvijas, again, who were given to untruth and injuring other creatures, possessed of cupidity, who indiscriminately followed all sorts of occupations for their maintenance, who had no purity of

---

[35] Prabhu, *Hindu Social Organization*, 292.

[36] Baker, *Caste*, 44-45.

behavior, and who thus nursed within the quality of darkness became Shudras.[37]

It has been shown that there were no restrictions in the Rigvedic society in the matter of diet and drink between the different Varnas such as we find in the later society. Whatever food or drink was usual was common to all the Varnas. So too, there was no 'higher' or 'lower' Varna for matrimonial alliance as the different groups in the society, whatever might be their occupations, were by complexion, features, language and creed practically homogeneous. Several instances of mixed marriages, occurring in the Rigvedic period and recorded in later literature, are in fact known to us – like those between Yayati, a Kshatriya king and Devayani, the daughter of a Brahmana sage.[38] From the above account during the vedic period, the Varnas seem to have been 'open classes'. They were not watertight compartments, the membership of which was determined by virtue of heredity only. Instead they were more based on individual traits and less upon descent.

Besides the four orders mentioned in the Rigveda, occupations like blacksmith, leather-worker, barber, physician, goldsmith, merchant, and chariot-builder too have been recorded. We do not know which of these occupations were comprised in any of the four orders, nor can we say that each of them constituted a separate class. Also in the Vedic literature the same occupation seems to have been given different names, either through individual or provincial peculiarities.[39]

We have seen that the three classes of the early portions of the Rigveda were later solidified into four groups which were nearly exclusive units. As far as religious and ritualistic life was concerned, only the first three orders were recognized. Though the Shudras were received within the precincts of the Aryan fold, they were systematically debarred from following the religious practices of the Aryans. Even the idea of Untouchability was first given literary

---

[37] Prabhu, *Hindu Social Organization*, 293.

[38] Prabhu, *Hindu Social Organization*, 288.

[39] Ghurye, *Caste and Class in India*, 52-53.

expression in connection with the Shudras and the sacrifice.[40] The Brahmanic literature of the post-Vedic period while stressing that there are only four Varnas also mentions certain mixed Castes (sankara Jati) and also a group of outcast classes (Antyavasayin).[41]

Among the four Varnas, the old distinction of Arya and Shudra later on appears predominantly as Dvija and Shudra. The first three Varnas are called Dvijas (twice-born) because they have to go through the initiation ceremony which is symbolic of rebirth. Since this privilege is denied to the Shudras they are called 'Ekajati' (once-birth). Though the word 'Jati' is used here for 'Varna' later on it is employed to mean the numerous sub-divisions of a Varna. It is also a vernacular term for a 'Caste.'[42] Thus, the Varna system became part and parcel of Hindu social order later degenerating into numerous Castes and sub-Castes.

1.2. The Origin of Castes – Varna Sankara

The word Caste was first used in India by the Portuguese to denote the several Jatis which they found existing here, and which have continued to exist since then, perhaps with addition.[43] The Varna theory of society is not to be confused with the Jati-system which we meet today in the Hindu society and which is usually described by the term 'Caste system'. The Castes and sub-Castes of the present day are considered derivative of the first four classes. This mixture of Castes (Varna system) is considered as an ideal necessity in the social organization of the Hindu Society.

According to Manu's theory of the origin of mixed Castes sons begotten by twice-born men (Dvijas, i.e., Brahamanas, Kshatriyas and Vaishyas) of wives from the immediate lower class belongs to the Varna of their fathers respectively. This law is applicable to children of a wife from a Varna only one degree lower than her husband's. The real 'mixture' of Varnas (Varna-sankara) arises with offspring born of a woman two or three degrees lower. Thus, the son born

---

[40] Ghurye, *Caste and Class in India*, 54-55.

[41] Ghurye, *Caste and Class in India*, 55.

[42] Ghurye, *Caste and Class in India*, 57.

[43] Prabhu, *Hindu Social Organization*, 297.

of a Brahmana father and a Vaishya mother would be called an Ambashtha; that born of a Brahmana father and a Shudra mother would be called Nishada, and so on. The mixture of Varnas takes place in other ways also. Offspring born of a Kshatriya father and Brahmana belong to the Suta Caste; children born of a Vaishya father and Kshatriya mother or a Brahmana mother belong to Magadha and Videha Castes respectively; and so on. Inter marriage between these new Castes give rise to newer and newer Castes, so that the process goes on multiplying.[44] Thus, the marriages between members of different Varna were 'anuloma' (hypergamous marriage in which the status of the bridegroom is higher socially than that of the bride) or 'pratiloma' (hypergamous marriage in which the status of the bride is socially higher than that of the bridegroom).[45]

In sloka (X, 11) Manu has used the word Jati as distinct from Varna. Thus the Suta, the Magagha and the Vaideha are so named according to their 'Jati'. Though Manu refers to four Varnas only, he mentions about fifty-seven Jatis, as a result of Varnas sankara.[46] From such mixed union between the different Varna, or between the Varna and the offspring of mixed unions and so forth come the various Castes of which 2378 were actually counted at the Indian census of 1901, some numbering millions, others only a very few individuals.[47]

It will not be an exaggeration to say that in India today there are probably 3000 Jatis (different Castes and sub-Castes) which are ranked in hierarchical order according to their social status. In general principle the pratiloma Castes rank below the anuloma, and at the bottom of the scale are the Chandala, begotten of a Shudra male and a Brahmin female, and other mixed Castes of Chandala parentage.[48]

After going through the above theory and explanation one might have realized that Caste is not an intellectual abstraction which may

---

[44] Prabhu, *Hindu Social Organization*, 296-297.

[45] J. H. Hutton, *Caste in India* (Bombay: Oxford University Press, 1963), 55.

[46] Prabhu, *Hindu Social Organization*, 296.

[47] Hutton, *Caste in India*, 149.

[48] Hutton, *Caste in India*, 55.

be exhaustively described by reference to the code of Manu or other ancient writings. Here, it emerges as a social form with a history of its own, which has changed, and is still changing. It has certainly diverged substantially from its misty and obscure origins and has developed into what it is today.

2. Difference between Caste and Varna

In vedic times the Varnas were classes rather than Castes and the post-vedic scholars, looking for authority for the Caste system in the earliest Vedas, have interpreted the nature of the Varna in terms of the Caste system as they knew it. At any rate the Varna of the present day is not a Caste, though it may be regarded as a group of Castes. There is a tendency among social reformers to advocate the substitution of four Varnas for three thousand or more endogamous groups of the Caste system.[49] This misunderstanding with regard to the inter-changeability of the terms 'Varna' and 'Caste' calls for further clarification of these terms.

Varna, like Caste, is to some extent fluid. Like Caste, it is an indeterminate expression, and persons belonging to one Varna in one locality may be otherwise classified in another. A person belonging to one Caste will always remain in that Caste irrespective of the place where one stays. Like Caste, Varna is also a variable social unit but it is wider and vaguer than Caste.[50]

The fundamental distinction between social class and Caste is more or less similar to the distinction between Varna and Jati. A Caste is a comparatively more rigid social class, to which transition from another class become well-nigh impossible.[51] The Varnas categorize various professions in a broad manner while within every Varna each Jati (sub-Caste) has its own particular profession limited to its own Caste members. Still, even if a person changes his profession, his Caste remains the same as before. The practice of Caste varies tremendously with area, and within specific regions it is more closely associated with Jati, or sub-Caste. Unlike the four

---

[49] Hutton, *Caste in India*, 66-67.

[50] Hutton, *Caste in India*, 67.

[51] Prabhu, *Hindu Social Organization*, 324.

Varnas, in any district there will not be just four Castes, but hundreds of endogamous sub-Castes.

Unlike the Varnas the Castes are endogamous in character. All Brahmins do not inter-marry, but there are many endogamous Brahmin Castes. There are very many Castes who claim Kshatriya origin and wear sacred thread of the twice-born, but do not inter-marry. Thus the Khatri, a Caste of the Punjab, of the United Provinces and of Bihar claiming Kshatriya origin, do not ordinarily inter-marry with Rajputs and indeed contain a number of endogamous sub-Castes. Thus, Varnas were basically classes rather than Castes in Vedic times.[52] The above account goes to show that the terms 'Varna' and 'Caste' are very much different from each other and hence are not interchangeable.

3. Features of the Caste System

The Hindu society is divided into groups, known as Castes, with varying degrees of respectability and circles of social intercourse. In fact, Caste is the most general form of social organization in India which presents a marked contrast to the social grouping prevalent in Europe or America. The outstanding features of Hindu society when it was ruled by the social philosophy of Caste, unaffected by the modern ideas of rights and duties, may be discerned to be six.

3.1. Segmental Division of Society

The Hindu Caste bound society was not a homogenous community and it had various groups with distinct appellations. Castes were groups with a well-developed life of their own, the membership whereof, unlike that of voluntary associations and of classes, was determined not by selection but by birth. The status of a person depended not on his wealth as in the classes of modern Europe, but on the traditional importance of Caste in which one was born. The Caste had a governing body called Panchayat which would deal with the offence of the members of the particular Caste. A Caste was a group with a separate arrangement for meting out justice to its members apart from that of the community as a whole, within

---

[52] Hutton, *Caste in India*, 66.

which the Caste was included as only one of the groups. Hence, the members of a Caste ceased to be members of the community as a whole, as far as that part of their morals which was regulated by law was concerned. Thus in this Caste-bound society the amount of community feeling was restricted, and the citizens owed moral allegiance to their Caste first, rather than to the community as a whole.[53]

The diversity in the administration of law necessarily led to difference in moral standards of the various Castes. A cultural gulf was thus created between the Castes. All these Castes differed from each other in their religious outlook. The customs about marriage and death varied widely among the different Caste. Brahmins did not permit widow-marriage nor tolerated concubinage as a Caste practice. This could not be said of many lower Castes. Not only were there such differences in cultural matters among the different Castes, but in theory also different standards of conduct were upheld. For their various affairs of day to day life the people required the co-operation of one's Caste people. Hence, Castes were small and complete social worlds in themselves, marked off definitely from one another, though subsisting within the larger society.[54]

3.2. Hierarchy

One of the principal characteristics of the Caste society was the hierarchy of the groups. Everywhere in India there was a definite scheme of social precedence amongst the Caste, with the Brahmin at the head of the hierarchy. In any one of the linguistic divisions of India there were as many as two hundred Castes which could be grouped in classes whose gradation was largely acknowledged by all. But the order of social precedence amongst the individual Castes of any class could not be made definite because not only was there no ungrudging acceptance of such rank but also the idea of people on this point were very nebulous and uncertain.[55]

---

[53] Ghurye, *Caste and Class in India*, 2-4.

[54] Ghurye, *Caste and Class in India*, 4-6.

[55] Ghurye, *Caste and Class in India*, 6-7.

3.3. Restrictions of Feeding and Social Intercourse

There were minute rules as to what sort of food or drink could be accepted by a person and from what Castes. However, there was a great diversity in this matter. The practices in the matter of food and social intercourse divided India into two broad belts.

In Hindustan proper,[56] Castes could be divided into five groups; first, the twice-born Caste, second, those Castes at whose hands the twice-born could take 'Pakka'[57] food; third, those Castes at whose hands the twice-born could not accept any kind of food but may take water; fourth, Castes that were not Untouchable yet were such that water from them could not be used by the twice-born; last come all those Castes whose touch defiled not only the twice-born but any orthodox Hindu.[58]

In the matter of food western Bengal resembled Hindustan except in this that in Bengal there were some people who would not accept 'Kachcha'[59] food even from the hands of a Brahmin. 'Pakka' food could be ordinarily taken not only from one's own or any higher Caste, but also from the lower Castes. As regards the position of the Untouchables- even the wells were polluted if a low Caste man drew water from them, but a great deal depended on the character of the vessel used and of the well from which the water was drawn. Certain low Castes were looked down upon as so unclean that they could not enter the courtyard of the great temples. These Castes were compelled to live by themselves on the outskirts of villages.[60]

---

[56] Hindustan proper = The Indo-Gangetic Plain, also known as the Indus-Ganga Plain and the North Indian River Plain, is a 255 million-hectare (630 million-acre) fertile plain encompassing most of northern and eastern India and the eastern parts of Pakistan.

[57] *Pakka* = food cooked in 'ghee' without the addition of water.

[58] Ghurye, *Caste and Class in India*, 7-8.

[59] *Kachcha* =food cooked in water.

[60] Ghurye, *Caste and Class in India*, 8-9.

3.4. Civil and Religious Disabilities and Privileges of the Different Sections

Segregation of individual Castes or of groups of Castes in a village was the most obvious mark of civil privileges and disabilities, and it prevailed in a more or less definite form all over India. Southern India, as in the matter of ceremonial purity and Untouchability, stood out distinct in their rigidity of these rules. In northern India it was impure Castes that were segregated and made to live in the outskirts of village. All over India the impure Castes were debarred from drawing water from the well, which was used by the members of other Castes. Besides this the lower Caste had to face disabilities with regards to their use of roads, schools, temples, clothes, ornaments and even the construction of their houses.[61]

3.5. Lack of Unrestricted Choice of Occupation

Generally a Caste or a group of allied Castes considered some of their callings (Caste-occupations) as their hereditary occupation and to abandon them in pursuit of another occupation was not thought to be right. Thus, a Brahmin thought that it was correct for him to be a priest, while the Chambhar regarded it as his duty to cure hides and prepare shoes. No Caste would allow its members to take to any occupation which was either degrading, like toddy-tapping and brewing, or impure, like scavenging or curing hides. It was not only the moral restraints and the social check of one's Caste-fellows that acted as a restraint on the choice of one's occupation, but also restriction put by other Castes, which did not allow members other than those of their own Caste to follow their occupations. The effect of these rules was that the priestly profession was entirely monopolized by the Brahmins, leaving aside the ministrants of the aboriginal deities, while they were seen plying trade which suited their tastes and which was not polluting.[62]

---

[61] Ghurye, *Caste and Class in India*, 10-15.

[62] Ghurye, *Caste and Class in India*, 15-17.

3.6. Restrictions on Marriage

Most of the Caste groups were further divided into a number of sub-groups everyone of which forbade its members to marry persons from outside it. Each sub-Caste was thus endogamous. This principle of strict endogamy was such a dominant aspect of Caste-society that an eminent sociologist was led to regard endogamy as 'the essence of the Caste system'. There were, however, a few exceptions to this general rule of marrying within one's own group which were due to practice of hypergamy (wherein a man of higher Caste takes a girl from lower Caste as his wife).[63]

---

[63] Ghurye, *Caste and Class in India*, 18.

Chapter 3

Ambedkar's Critique of Traditional Hindu Social Order

In the previous chapter I have explained how the four Varnas originated and how the Castes came to be through the principle of Varna Sankara. I have also considered the difference between Caste and Varna and the various features of the Caste system.

Ambedkar's formal education, world travel, personal experience of Untouchable society, and the Indian independence movement spearheaded by the Congress leaders, drawn from top Caste groups, provided ample opportunity to him to reflect on the Hindu social organization. Throughout his life he was engaged in exposing the evil effects of the Hindu social order. He realized the need to reach the roots and to search for the causes of these social evils, so as to abolish them.

The task of this chapter is, therefore, to elaborate in detail Ambedkar's critique of traditional Hindu social order, by highlighting the salient features of his social philosophy. I shall do it in two sections. The first section will focus in a rather lengthy manner on Ambedkar's presentation of the Varna and the Caste system and how it led to the degradation of the Shudra and the Untouchables. The second section deals with Ambedkar's efforts to eliminate social evils of the Caste and the Varna system and to liberate Hindu women.

1. Caste and Untouchability according to Ambedkar

Ambedkar was well aware of the importance of Varna and Castes in the Hindu social order. He realized the inequality and inhumanity that they perpetuated in the existing social order. His critique of the Hindu social order is in fact geared towards the exposure of its lack of spirit of humanism which creates the feeling of love, good-will and brotherhood among people. In this section I have highlighted his critical evaluation about the Varna and the Caste system and how they gave rise to the servile classes – namely the Shudras and the Untouchables.

1.1. The Origin of the Shudras

Everyone today knows about the Shudras as the fourth Varna of the Chaturvarnya theory of the Indo-Aryan society. However, very few people have cared to find out who the Shudras were and how they came to be the fourth Varna of the Indo-Aryan society. The most prominent among them is Dr. Ambedkar, who has put light on this issue by giving us a detailed account of the origin of the Shudra.

The Purusha Sukta, a part of the Rig Veda, is considerd as 'unique' because of its theory of Chaturvarnya, which is held as the ideal of social organization.[64] This Chaturvarnya theory distinguishes the four Varnas, namely (a) Brahmins or priest (b) Kshatriyas or soldiers (c) Vaishyas or traders and (d) Shudras or menials. They are divinely ordained and have their own duties in a hierarchical order.[65]

The view of the Purusha Sukta concerning the origin of the Shudra, is that from the beginning, there had been four Varnas. But Ambedkar refutes this theory by saying that at first there were only three Varnas – Brahmin, Kshatriya and Vaishya, and the Shudras were really Kshatriyas, who lost their social status in the supremacy against the Brahmins. It is the Purusha Sukta, which refers to and justifies

---

[64] B.R. Ambedkar, "The Riddle of the Shudras" *Writings and Speeches – Vol. 7* (Bombay: The Education Department - Government of Maharashtra, 1990), 23.

[65] Ambedkar, "The Riddle of the Shudras" 23.

the existence of the fourth Varna, i.e., the Shudras. Ambedkar shows us that Purusha Sukta is an interpolation which has taken place long after the Rig Veda was closed.[66]

According to Ambedkar, this Purusha Sukta is full of 'riddles'. In his view the ideals as norms are good and necessary for the society and the individual, but they must change with time and circumstances. He observes that the Purusha Sukta, makes the Chaturvarnya a 'sacred institution', a 'divine ordination'. Why is this social order made so 'sacred' as to be beyond criticism and beyond change?[67] This is the first 'riddle' of the Purusha Sukta.

The Purusha Sukta, Ambedkar continues, in propounding the doctrine of Chaturvarnya, plays a double role. It proceeds first 'to raise the real', namely, the existence of the four classes in the Indo-Aryan society, 'to the status of an ideal'. He calls it a deception because 'the ideal is in no way different from facts as they exist'. After raising 'the real to the status of an ideal', it proceeds 'to make a show of giving effect to what it regards as an ideal'. This, again, he sees as a deception because 'the ideal already exists in fact'. Such an attempt 'to idealize the real and to realize the ideal', is a kind of political jugglery, which is against the principle of morality. It means perpetuating inequality on the grounds that whatever is once settled, is settled for all times. Ambedkar argues that whatever progress in improving the terms of associated life between individuals and classes has been made in the course of history is due, entirely, to the recognition of the ethical doctrine that 'what is wrongly settled is never settled and must be resettled'. Why does the Purusha Sukta play a double role?[68] This is the second riddle.

On the point of the origin of the four Varnas, the Purusha Sukta declares that they were created by 'God' by equating these Varnas with the different parts of the creator's body. Ambedkar observes that in doing so, it plays a double role at the same time by 'fixing the

---

[66] B.R. Ambedkar, "The Number of Varnas, Three or Four" *Writings and Speeches – Vol. 7* (Bombay: The Education Department - Government of Maharashtra, 1990), 132.

[67] Ambedkar, "The Riddle of the Shudras" 31.

[68] Ambedkar, "The Riddle of the Shudras" 31-32.

function as well as the gradation of the four classes'. Why are these classes equated with the body of the creator, and why did it equate the Shudras to the feet?[69] This is the important riddle as it is the one relating to the position of the Shudras. The greatest of all the riddles, according to Ambedkar, is 'the separation of the Shudras from the first three Varnas.'[70] i.e. Although being part of the Chaturvarnya system, the Shudras unlike the first three Varnas, were not allowed to receive the 'Upanayana ceremony.'[71] It calls for an investigation and an explanation of the origin of the Shudras and how they came to be the fourth Varna.

According to Ambedkar, the origin of the Shudras may be traced to the well-known struggle for supremacy that took place in the ancient past, between the Brahmins and the Kshatriyas. It is connected to the rivalry between two priests – Vasistha a 'Brahmin priest' and Visvamitra a 'Kshatriya priest' – as regard the priority of superiority they claimed in the matters relating to the institution of priesthood.[72] King Sudas, a Kshatriya king, played an important part in the dispute between Vasistha and Vishvamitra. He removed Vasistha, his family priest, from his office and appointed Visvamitra in his place. According to Satyayana Brahmana, Sudas also threw into the fire Shakti, the son of Vasistha, and burned him alive. As a result the enmity between the Brahmana priest and the Shudras, the followers of King Sudas, reached its heights. In the spirit of taking revenge, the Brahmins not only degraded the progeny of Sudas to menial ranks, but also prevented them from taking Upanayana ceremony which wrecked the Shudras completely.[73]

---

[69] Ambedkar, "The Riddle of the Shudras" 32-33.

[70] Ambedkar, "The Riddle of the Shudras" 36.

[71] *Upanayana* ceremony = it is an initiation ceremony where a boy is given right to wear the sacred thread. Though this process he is initiated into the class of 'twice-born' and is made eligible for the study of the Vedas.

[72] B.R. Ambedkar, "Brahmins *Versus* Shudras" *Writings and Speeches – Vol. 7* (Bombay: The Education Department - Government of Maharashtra, 1990), 140-154.

[73] B.R. Ambedkar, "The Degradation of the Shudras" *Writings and Speeches – Vol. 7* (Bombay: The Education Department - Government of Maharashtra, 1990), 156-161.

This ban against 'Upanayana' to all the Shudras was so great that it divided the Shudras – progeny of king Sudas – not only from their own Kshatriyas community, but also from all other three Varna communities by regarding them as a separate community altogether. Ambedkar observes that Manu, in the later ancient period, 'to realize the ideal' invested the social code of Chaturvarnya contained in the Purusha Sukta, with a degree of 'divinity and infallibility' which it did not have before.[74] Thus, the Shudras became the most degraded people, the fourth Varna of Chaturvarnya occupying the lowest rung of the social ladder.

According to Ambedkar, in modern times, the word 'Shudras' has acquired a different meaning in Hindu society. It was a proper name of one person belonging to the solar race in the Indo-Aryans society. Now it has been associated with the 'low uncultured class of people', which is miscellaneous and heterogeneous collection of tribes and groups that have nothing in common except existence on the lower plane of culture.[75] They have very little to do with the original Shudras. It is therefore wrong to call them by name of the Shudras or to punish them for the crime they have not done.

Ambedkar's theory of the origin of the Shudras may be summarized as follows:

1. The Shudras were one of the Aryan communities of the solar race.
2. There was a time when the Aryan society recognized three Varnas, namely, Brahmins, Kshatriyas and Vaishyas.
3. The Shudras did not form a separate Varna. They ranked as part of the Kshatriya Varna in the Indo-Aryan society.
4. There was a continuous feud between the Shudra kings and the Brahmins in which the Brahmins were subjected to many tyrannies and oppressions.
5. As a result of the hatred towards the Shudras generated by their tyrannies and oppressions, the Brahmins refused to perform the Upanayana of the Shudras.

---

[74] Ambedkar, "The Riddle of the Shudras" 31.

[75] Jatava, *The Social Philosophy of B.R. Ambedkar,* 52.

6. Owing to the denial of Upanayana, the Shudras who were Kshatriyas became socially degraded, fell below the rank of the Vaishyas and thus came to form the fourth Varna.[76]

1.2. The Origin of the Untouchables

That the Untouchables live outside the village is a known fact to everyone. However, how did the Untouchables come to live outside the village? If they were living outside the village from the very beginning, what can be the reason for it? Ambedkar here proposes a theory with regard to the origin of the Untouchables and further explains as to why they were treated as Outcastes and Untouchables.

According to Ambedkar, it is necessary for us to understand that the modern society differs from primitive society in two respects. (i) Primitive society consisted of 'nomadic communities' while modern society consists of 'settled communities'. (ii) Primitive society consisted of 'tribal communities' based on 'blood relationship' while modern society consists of 'local communities' based on 'territorial affiliation'. Thus, primitive society evolved in two ways – from a 'tribal' to a 'territorial' community and from 'nomadic' to a 'settled' community.[77]

Primitive society was nomadic due to the fact that cattle were held as wealth by it. The primitive people had to go around with their cattle from place to place. When 'land' was discovered as a new form of wealth, they became a 'settled community'. They learned the 'art' of farming and of 'cultivating land'. Thus when the wealth was fixed at one place in the form of 'land', instead of 'cattle' the primitive society became settled at the same place.[78]

According to Ambedkar the transformation of the primitive society from nomadic to the life of a settled community, was marked by two important features:

---

[76] B.R. Ambedkar, "Preface" *Writings and Speeches – Vol. 7* (Bombay: The Education Department - Government of Maharashtra, 1990), 11-12.

[77] B.R. Ambedkar, "Why do the Untouchables live outside the Village?" *Writings and Speeches – Vol. 7* (Bombay: The Education Department - Government of Maharashtra, 1990), 273.

[78] Ambedkar, "Why do the Untouchables live outside the Village?" 274.

i) Since all the tribes in primitive society could not settle at one place at the same time, the 'settled' tribes faced the danger of raids from the envious 'nomadic' tribes. Secondly, the settled tribes were always at war with each other.

ii) Sometimes, a settled tribe was defeated and routed by the organized raids and became broken into bits. Without wealth and goods, they roamed astray in all directions to become the group of people known as the 'broken men'.

These broken men were always in danger of being attacked since they could not join any other primitive tribes which were based on common blood and kinship relations. So there arose the problems of food, shelter and protection for these 'broken men.'[79]

The 'broken men' therefore made a 'bargain' with the settled tribe, whereby they would 'watch and ward' for settled tribes against the raiders and in turn they would get food and shelter from them. There arose the problems of settlement of these 'broken men' among the settled people. The solution was found by allowing these 'broken men' to live on the outskirts of the village, whereby they could check the raids of the hostile tribes, and at the same time, could remain outside the 'blood relationship.'[80] Due to this subordinate social position of the 'broken men', inter-dining and inter-marriage were not possible between these two groups of people. According to Ambedkar, the same process must have taken place in the Primitive Hindu Society where the 'broken men' living away from the village community eventually became the Untouchables.[81]

To support his theory of the Untouchables as originally being the 'broken men', Ambedkar gives us two sets of evidentiary facts.

i) One set of facts consists of the names 'Antya', 'Antyaja' and 'Antyavasin' given to certain communities in the Hindu Shastras. They are derived from the root 'Anta'. According to Shastra it means one who is born last and as the Untouchable. Ambedkar refutes this view saying, that, according to the

[79] Ambedkar, "Why do the Untouchables live outside the Village?" 274-276.

[80] Ambedkar, "Why do the Untouchables live outside the Village?" 276.

[81] Ambedkar, "Why do the Untouchables live outside the Village?" 277.

> Hindu theory of 'Divine Creation' it is the Shudra, not the Untouchable, who is born last. The Untouchables are outside this theory for they are called 'Avarna' i.e., outside the Varnas. Therefore, the Hindu theory of 'Divine Creation' cannot be applied to the Untouchables.[82]

Ambedkar further explains that the word 'Antya' means the end of the 'Hindu village system' and not the end of the 'Divine Creation'. It was a name given to those people who lived outside the village, i.e., on the 'Antya' of the village and were thus called 'Antyaja' or 'Antyavasin'. The use of these words has a double significance. a) That living in separate quarters was such a 'peculiar phenomenon' that a new terminology had to be invented to give expression to it. b) That the words chosen to express, in exact terms, the condition of the people to whom it applied, namely, was 'aliens.'[83]

ii) The second set of facts which shows that the Untouchables were 'broken men' relates to the Mahars of Maharashtra – the single largest community of the Untouchables. The relations between the Mahars and the Touchable are noteworthy:

a) The Mahars are to be found in every village;
b) Every village in Maharashtra has a wall and the Mahars have their quarters outside the wall;
c) The Mahars by turn do the duty of watch and ward on behalf of the village; and
d) The Mahars claims 52 rights against the Hindu villagers.[84]

Ambedkar observes that if such evidence is taken as typical of Untouchables throughout India, it should be accepted that there was a stage in the history of India when the 'broken men' belonging to other tribes came to be settled tribes and struck a bargain, whereby

---

[82] B.R. Ambedkar, "Are the Untouchables Broken Men?" *Writings and Speeches – Vol. 7* (Bombay: The Education Department - Government of Maharashtra, 1990), 278-279.

[83] Ambedkar, "Are the Untouchables Broken Men?", 279.

[84] Ambedkar, "Are the Untouchables Broken Men?", 279.

the 'broken men' were allowed to settle on the 'outskirts' of the Hindu village.[85]

These two sets of facts do give us some evidence in support of the theory that the Untouchables lived outside the village from the beginning, because they were 'broken men' who belonged to a tribe different from the other settled tribes.

Ambedkar also narrates two parallel cases of 'broken men' in the writing of Sir Henry Maine and Mr. Seebhans. They are the 'Fuidhirs of Ireland' and the 'Alltudes of Wales.'[86] At some stage, Ambedkar observes, there came into being in primitive society a 'rule of ennoblement' whereby a non-tribesmen could become the member of the tribe and become absorbed in it as a kindred. This helped the Fuidhir of Ireland and the Alltudes of Wales to become absorbed in other tribes as their kindred.[87]

As Ambedkar observes, this did not happen in India because the notion of Untouchability perpetuated the differences between the Touchables and the Untouchables, preventing the social assimilation of the Untouchables – the 'broken men'– with the tribesmen of the village proper. As a result, the system of separate quarters became a perpetual and a permanent feature of Indian villages.[88]

Ambedkar does not stop here with his explanation of the origin of the Untouchables, but goes further to understand how the 'notion of Untouchability' came into being. In the process he negates some old theories with regard to the origin of Untouchability and presents his own new theories with reasonable explanation.

It is quite surprising to see that apart from Rice, no other sociologist has attempted to explain how Untouchability has come

---

85 Ambedkar, "Are the Untouchables Broken Men?", 279.

86 B.R. Ambedkar, "Are there Parallel Cases?" *Writings and Speeches – Vol. 7* (Bombay: The Education Department - Government of Maharashtra, 1990), 281-283. Both 'Fuidhirs of Ireland' and the 'Alltudes of Wales' were considered to be broken men in their respective countries.

87 B.R. Ambedkar, "How did Separate Settlements for Broken Men disappear elsewhere?" *Writings and Speeches – Vol. 7* (Bombay: The Education Department - Government of Maharashtra, 1990), 284-285.

88 Ambedkar, "How did Separate Settlements for Broken Men disappear elsewhere?" 285.

about. According to Stanley Rice, the origin of Untouchability is to be found in two circumstances – Race and Occupation.[89] His racial theory of the origin of Untouchability contains two elements: i) That the Untouchables are non-Aryans, non-Dravidian aboriginals; and ii) that they were conquered and subjugated by the Dravidians.

Although the theory holds that the Untouchables, non-Dravidians aboriginals, were conquered by Dravidians, the Dravidians too were later conquered by the Aryans. However, he does not mention how the conquering Aryans treated the conquered Dravidians. Ambedkar believes, if pressed for an answer he might say, they made them Shudras, which provides the missing link in the chain of events. Besides, this theory raises the whole question of the invasion of India by foreign invaders, the conquests made by them and the social and cultural institutions that have resulted from it.[90] Since this racial theory does not suffice to answer these questions, to Ambedkar's mind it is of no use and therefore is to be abandoned.

According to the occupational theory of Untouchability, the clue is to be found in the unclean filthy occupations of the Untouchables. Ambedkar argues that, the filthy and unclean occupations which the Untouchables perform are common to all the human societies and there are people who perform these occupations. Why are such people not treated as Untouchables in other parts of the world? Secondly, there is no evidence on the point that the Dravidians had nausea against persons engaged in them. Even the Brahmins, the Kshatriyas and the Vaishyas do the work of scavengers, which is the filthiest of filthy occupations. If scavenging was not loathsome to these people, how can it be said that engaging in filthy occupations is the cause of Untouchability? This theory is, therefore, untenable.[91]

---

[89] B.R. Ambedkar, "Racial Difference as the Origin of Untouchability" *Writings and Speeches – Vol. 7* (Bombay: The Education Department - Government of Maharashtra, 1990), 290.

[90] Ambedkar, "Racial Difference as the Origin of Untouchability" 290-291.

[91] B.R. Ambedkar, "Occupational Origin of Untouchability" *Writings and Speeches – Vol. 7* (Bombay: The Education Department - Government of Maharashtra, 1990), 305-307.

Ambedkar, then, presents these new theories of the origin of Untouchability. They are: Contempt for Buddhism as the root of Untouchability and Beef-eating as the root of Untouchability.

i) Contempt for Buddhism as the Root of Untouchability:

Ambedkar observes that for the first time, the Census Report for the year 1910 divided the Hindus under three separate categories: a) Hindus b) Animists and Tribal People, and c) Depressed classes or the Untouchables. The division was made on the basis of (i) those who were hundred percent Hindus and (ii) those who were not hundred percent Hindus, the lower Caste people.

The points on which the Census Commissioners of all Provinces were unanimous are: a) That the Untouchables do not receive mantra from a Brahmin. b) That the Untouchables are not served by good Brahmin priests, and c) That the Untouchables have their own priests prepared from themselves.[92]

The inquiries of the Census Commissioners were one sided and failed to explain the origin of Untouchability because they only showed that the Brahmans shunned the Untouchables. According to Ambedkar, they did not bring to light the fact that the Untouchables also shunned the Brahmins.[93]

According to Ambedkar, this 'antipathy' between the Brahmin and the 'broken men' (the Untouchables), can be explained on one hypothesis. "It is that the 'broken men' were Buddhist."[94] As such they did not revere the Brahmins, did not employ them as their priests and regarded them as impure. The Brahmins on the other hand disliked the 'broken men' because they were Buddhists and preached against them contempt and hatred. As a result the 'broken men' came to be regarded as Untouchables by the Brahmins.[95]

If this hypothesis is accepted then we have a plausible explanation as to why the 'broken men' came to be regarded as Untouchables.

---

[92] B.R. Ambedkar, "Contempt for Buddhists as the Root of Untouchability" *Writings and Speeches – Vol. 7* (Bombay: The Education Department - Government of Maharashtra, 1990), 311-313.

[93] Ambedkar, "Contempt for Buddhists as the Root of Untouchability" 314.

[94] Ambedkar, "Contempt for Buddhists as the Root of Untouchability" 315.

[95] Ambedkar, "Contempt for Buddhists as the Root of Untouchability" 315.

The Brahmins shunned the 'broken men' due to their acceptance of Buddhism and because of the Brahmins enmity towards Buddhism, they were hated by the 'broken men'. It is on this reasoning that Ambedkar concludes: "One of the roots of Untouchability lies in the hatred and contempt, which the Brahmins created against those who were Buddhists."[96]

ii) Beef Eating as the Root cause of Untouchability:

Another important reason for the 'broken men' to be treated as Untouchables is their continuation of the habit of 'beef-eating'. According to Ambedkar, there was a time when the Hindus - both Brahmins and non-Brahmins - ate not only meat, but also beef.[97] In ancient times, animal sacrifices being part of the religious rites, the Brahmin priest would get beef to eat almost every day. The cow being a costly animal, the non-Brahmins could afford to slaughter it only on special occasions when they had to perform religious duties.[98]

With the rise of Buddhism, which preached ahimsa, a strong feeling of reverence towards all servient beings was created in the mind of people. This prohibition attracted many 'broken men' who were disrespected and ill-treated by the village community. The deep impressions of Buddhist doctrine on their mind eventually led them to embrace Buddhism. They thus began to criticize Brahmanism for its sacrifices.[99] Thus, Brahmanism suffered in esteem at the hands of Buddhism.

To regain their social positions against the rising influence of the Buddhists, the Brahmins gave up the Yajna as a form of worship and the sacrifice of the cow. They also made the cow as a sacred animal by starting cow-worship. Killing of cows was regarded as a mortal

---

[96] Ambedkar, "Contempt for Buddhists as the Root of Untouchability" 317.

[97] B.R. Ambedkar, "Did the Hindus never eat Beef?" *Writings and Speeches – Vol. 7* (Bombay: The Education Department - Government of Maharashtra, 1990), 328.

[98] B.R. Ambedkar, "What made the Brahmins become Vegetarians?" *Writings and Speeches – Vol. 7* (Bombay: The Education Department - Government of Maharashtra, 1990), 348.

[99] Ambedkar, "What made the Brahmins become Vegetarians?" 345-46.

sin and capital offence was sanctioned and recognized for those who went against it.[100]

The 'broken men' could not adhere to this rule and continued to eat beef, which resulted in their treatment as the 'Untouchables' (unfit for association) by the Brahmins. The reason for continuing the practice of beef-eating was that they had no other means for their livelihood apart from depending upon the dead cow or any other animal. Being 'broken men' they had neither land nor cattle. They, therefore earned their livelihood by carrying on business with the dead cow's skin, bones, flesh, etc., which was the only source of their support.[101] Thus, because of their practice of beef-eating, the 'broken men' came to be regarded as the Untouchables.

1.3. The Essential Character of the Caste System

So far I have tried to show how Ambedkar, while criticizing Caste, rejected the old theories of the origin of the Shudras and the Untouchables and substituted them with his own. In this section he continues his attack on the Caste system. In the process he evaluates various theories and definitions of Caste by eminent sociologists and exposes their shortcomings. He then comes up with his own explanation of the Caste system with 'endogamy' as its essential characteristic.

The Caste problem in India is a vast complicated one, both theoretically and practically. Practically it is an institution that portends tremendous consequences. Though it appears to be a local problem, it is capable of creating wider tensions, for "as long as Caste in India does exist, Hindus will hardly inter-marry or have any social intercourse with outsiders; and if Hindus migrate to other regions in the world, Indian Castes would become a world problem."[102] Many scholars have theoretically tried to investigate its cause. As Ambedkar will show, most of them have mistaken mere description

[100] Ambedkar, "What made the Brahmins become Vegetarians?" 348.

[101] B.R. Ambedkar, "Why should Beef-eating make Broken Men Untouchables?" *Writings and Speeches – Vol. 7* (Bombay: The Education Department - Government of Maharashtra, 1990), 353-55.

[102] B.R. Ambedkar, "Castes in India" *Writings and Speeches – Vol. 1* (Bombay: The Education Department - Government of Maharashtra, 1979), 5-6.

for explanation of the origin of Castes. He advances further to show us the real essence of the origin of the Caste system.

Ambedkar here quotes few social investigators with their various definition of Caste:

1. Mr. Émile Charles Marie Senart, a French Indologist, defines a Caste as "a close corporation, in theory at any rate rigorously hereditary; equipped with a certain traditional and independent organization, including a chief and a council, meeting on occasions in assemblies of more or less plenary authority and joining together at certain festivals; bound together by common occupations, which relate more particularly to marriage and its members by the exercise of jurisdiction, the extent of which varies, but which succeeds in making the authority of the community more felt by the sanction of certain penalties and, above all, by final irrevocable exclusion from the group."[103]
2. John Collinson Nesfield, an educator in British India, defines a Caste as "a class of the community which disowns any connection with any other class and can neither inter-marry nor eat nor drink with any persons of their community."[104]
3. According to Sir Herbert Hope Risley, a British ethnographer and colonial administrator, "a Caste may be defined as a collection of families or groups bearing a common name which usually denotes or is associated with specific occupation, claiming common descent from mythical ancestor, human or divine, professing to follow the same professional callings and are regarded by those who are competent to give an opinion as forming a single homogenous community."[105]
4. Dr. S. V. Ketkar, a noted sociologist, historian and novelist from Maharashtra , defines Caste as "a social group having two characteristics: (i) Membership is confined to those who

[103] Ambedkar, "Castes in India" 6-7.

[104] Ambedkar, "Castes in India" 7.

[105] Ambedkar, "Castes in India" 7.

> are born of members and includes all persons so born; (ii) The members are forbidden by an inexorable social law to marry outside the group."[106]

According to Ambedkar, if the definitions by these scholars are taken individually they seem to include too much or too little. None is complete by itself and all have missed the central point in the mechanism of the Caste system. They have been mistaken by trying to define Caste as an isolated unit by itself, and not as a group within, and with definite relation to, the system of Caste as a whole. Yet collectively, all of their views are complementary to each other, each one emphasizing what has been obscured in the other. By way of criticism, therefore, Ambedkar examines only these points common to all in each of the above definitions, which are regarded as peculiarities of Caste.[107]

To start with Senart, he expresses the 'idea of pollution' as a characteristic of Caste. As for Ambedkar this idea of pollution has very little to do with the origin of Caste, because it is related to only the priestly class to whom the notion of purity and impurity is associated. For Nasfield, the absence of messing with those outside the Caste is the cause of Caste. As Ambedkar points out rightly, Nesfield has mistaken the effect for the cause, because the absence of general messing system is a natural result of the Caste mechanism, i.e., exclusiveness, but not the cause of it. According to him, Sir H. Risely makes no new point deserving of special attention. Dr. Ketkar's definition merits consideration for he has defined Caste in its relation to a system of Caste by concentrating his attention only on the characteristics absolutely necessary for the existence of a Caste within a system. Yet, Ambedkar finds a slight confusion in his thought. He speaks of 'Prohibition of Intermarriage and Membership by Autogeny' as the two characteristics of Caste. Thus Ambedkar says, these two aspects are one and the same things and not two different things as Dr. Ketkar supposes them to be. Further

---

[106] Ambedkar, "Castes in India" 7.

[107] Ambedkar, "Castes in India" 7.

the prohibition of inter-marriage results in limited membership to those born within the group.[108]

Dr. Ambedkar regards endogamy, or the absence of intermarriage as the only trait that can be called the essence of the Caste system. He proceeds further to give his reason for it. Though other countries too have homogeneous people, Indian homogeneous population stands separate from them because by Indian society 'the rule of endogamy' is a creed and nobody dares to infringe it. Although, the rule of exogamy seems to be a positive injunction for all practical purposes, it is the superimposition of endogamy on exogamy that leads to the creation of a Caste. The other societies do not have hard and fast rule regarding the marriage system. That is why according to Ambedkar 'the rule of endogamy' is largely responsible for the 'Caste mechanism.'[109]

According to Ambedkar it is Manu who is responsible for the creation of Castes though his laws. He codified the rules for the marriages and gave them 'religious sanction', i.e., not to marry outside one's group, class or Varna. The breaking of this rule was considered to be a sin against Divine will and the penalties were given for the law breaker. Thus through the law of endogamy Manu strengthens the Caste system.[110]

To check the 'exogamous' tendencies of people, the penalty imposed for the violation of the rule, was the 'excommunication' of an individual from the main class. These excommunicated people formed the separate 'enclosed group' resulting into a new Caste. With the lapse of time, there was further fragmentation of the enclosed groups creating groups within groups, i.e., Castes within Castes. Thus with the breaking of the rule of endogamy, the process of Caste formation took place in India.[111]

In conclusion, it is the struggle for supremacy between the different classes in Indian Society that led to the formation of the Caste system and the origin of servile classes as the Shudras and the

---

[108] Ambedkar, "Castes in India" 7-8.

[109] Ambedkar, "Castes in India" 8-9.

[110] Ambedkar, "Castes in India" 16.

[111] Ambedkar, "Castes in India" 20.

Untouchables. This type of social order lacked social harmony in the society. Values such as democracy, liberty, equality, fraternity were not cared for. Millions of men and women belonging to lower Castes were denied the basic human rights such as education, property and arms. This resulted into degradation of human order, perpetual inhuman treatment by upper classes towards the Untouchables and the Shudras and the development of spirit of separation, hatred and enmity between all the existing classes.

The experience of this situation in his early life later developed a strong urge for social change in Ambedkar. He therefore stood firm, almost single handed, for a radical change so as to establish right relation among men in Indian society.

2. Ambedkar's Quest for a New Social Order

Ambedkar, throughout his life, was exposed to the social evils of the Caste system. He therefore sought to destroy the belief in Shastras, which is the basis of the so divinely ordained Varnas and Castes. To eliminate the rule of 'endogamy' which gave rise to the various Castes and sub-Castes, he strives for 'intermarriages' between the members of those Castes and sub-Castes. In this section I will examine Ambedkar's strategy to eliminate Varnas and Castes and to liberate women from their bondage, which will be a stepping stone towards the fulfillment of his dream of creation of a new social order.

2.1. The Rejection of the Varna System

As I have already shown, the Hindu social order degenerated into an instrument of exploitation, tyranny and oppression, because of which many people were deprived of their basic human rights such as education and property. Thus it tended to perpetuate inequality and inhumanity among people. Ambedkar holds the Varna system responsible for such a state of human affair in Indians society. Here, he makes an effort to explain the inherent social evil in the Varna system and the need to change it for the betterment of the society today.

Ambedkar finds many lamentable rigidities in the Varna system of Hindu social organization of which a few can be mentioned here:

(i) Although every society recognizes the existence of classes the Hindu theory of Chaturvarnya is the only instance in which 'the real is elevated to the dignity of the ideal'.

(ii) Though Plato's class composition was put as ideal, the Greeks never gave a law sanction to it to make it real. However, in Hindu society an attempt was made 'to give reality to the ideal by invoking the sanction of the law'.

(iii) Unlike the other societies, the theory of Chaturvarnya makes the division of society into four classes 'a matter of inalterable dogma'.

(iv) People in the other societies have accepted the class composition as being natural and never as an ideal. In Hindu social organization 'the class composition is considered not only as natural but also as sacred and divine'.

(v) Every society leaves a class to find its own place among other classes, as the human need dictate. However, the social ideal of Chaturvarnya gives 'an official gradation, fixation and permanency to each Varna on the principle of graded inequality in society.'[112]

For the justification of this social scheme, Purusha Sukta is held as an original source. Later on it was upheld on the principle of the gunas, determining individual's inclination towards one of the four broad groups of vocations and duties. Ambedkar argues that if each person, according to guna theory, has three gunas i.e. sattva, rajas, tamas, of which anyone can dominate at any time, then the character of a person will always be in the process of change with the changing position of the gunas. Therefore, how can we hold that a particular guna dominating in a particular person at the time of birth continues to dominate throughout his life till his death? Ambedkar thinks that

---

[112] B.R. Ambedkar, "Annihilation of Caste" The speech prepared for the 1936 Annual Conference of the Jat-Pat-todak Mandal of Lahore but not delivered owing to the cancellation of the Conference by the Reception Committee on the ground that the views expressed in the Speech would be unbearable to the Conference. *Writings and Speeches – Vol. 1* (Bombay: The Education Department - Government of Maharashtra, 1979), 60-63.

there is no basis for such assumption since all our experience, mental states, as also the happening of the nature, are changeable.[113]

According to the defender of the Varna system, it is but another name for the division of labour, and since division of labour is a necessary feature of every civilized society, there is nothing wrong in the social organization of Chaturvarnya. To them Ambedkar makes it clear that Varna system is not merely a division of labour but it is a division of labourers. Further, it is a hierarchy in which the division of labourers is graded one above the other.[114]

Besides, this division of labour is not based on choice or on individual preference but it is based on the dogma of 'predestination'. Therefore, for Ambedkar, the greatest evil in the Hindu social order is not so much the 'property' and 'suffering' that it involves, but the psychological tragedy of 'hereditary callings' (Jati-occupations), which make no appeal to the conscience of those who are engaged in them. Such callings constantly provoke one to aversion, ill-will and the desire to evade work. Many occupations in Hindu society are regarded as low. Those engaged in them are regarded as degraded people; they consequently wish to evade work and escape from such occupation. What efficiency can there be in a system under which neither people's hearts nor their minds are in their work?[115]

This social stratification created through this Varna system, in Ambedkar's opinion, is not suited to the needs of the time. To match the rapid and abrupt changes in industry, he remarks, the individual must be left free to change his occupation. Without such freedom to adjust himself to changing circumstances it would be impossible for him to gain his livelihood.[116] As an economic organization, the Varna system is, therefore, in Ambedkar's view, a 'harmful institution', In as

---

[113] D.R. Jatava, *The Social Philosophy of B.R. Ambedkar* (Agra: Phoenix Publication House, 1965), 74-75.

[114] Ambedkar, "Annihilation of Caste" 47.

[115] Ambedkar, "Annihilation of Caste" 47-48.

[116] Ambedkar, "Annihilation of Caste" 47-48.

much as, it involves the subordination of man's natural 'powers' and 'inclinations' to the exigencies of social rules.[117]

In defense of the Varna system, it is said that the object of this social stratification has been to preserve the 'purity of race or blood' of the upper classes. Ambedkar disagrees with this view saying that the ethnologists of today are of the opinion that people of pure race exist nowhere and that there has been a mixture of all races in all parts of the world. There is hardly a class in India, he observes, which has not a foreign stain in it. He further adds, the Brahmin of Madras is of the same race as the pariah of Madras. The Varna system thus does not demarcate any racial division. The purpose of this social division of people of the same race is just to preserve the status group and not the purity of race or blood.[118]

Some uphold the dignity of the Varna system by arguing that it is the best possible means for securing 'social stability'. Ambedkar find faults with such stability for although people are anxious for social stability they would not want it to be based on static relationship or something that is inalterable. He says that stability is wanted but not at the cost of change when change is imperative; social adjustment is required but not at the sacrifice of social justice.[119] He therefore urges people to do with the theory of Chaturvarnya, which is based on hereditary callings.

Ambedkar observes that along with each Varna there are innumerable Castes and sub-Castes. Caste and Varna are two different things. While Caste is based on 'birth', Varna may be based on 'worth' under ideal conditions. He therefore asks: "How are we going to compel people to recognize the status due to a man in accordance with his worth, when he is occupying a lower status based on his birth? For this we must break up the Caste system, in order to be able to establish the Varna system."[120] In Ambedkar's opinion it is something impractical to reduce the thousands of Castes into the four Varnas in accordance with the merits and demerits of

---

[117] Jatava, *The Social Philosophy of B.R. Ambedkar,* 77.

[118] Ambedkar, "Annihilation of Caste" 48-49.

[119] Jatava, *The Social Philosophy of B.R. Ambedkar,* 77-78.

[120] Ambedkar, "Annihilation of Caste" 50.

each individual. He thus brings out the inherent contradiction in the Hindu social system with regards to its practice of Caste and Varna system.

It is because of such evil nature of Chaturvarnya system that Ambedkar sought to change it. He makes us aware that the historical significance of the ideal of Chaturvarnya has out-grown its utility. He expresses the need to destroy this social ideal of Chaturvarnya by its roots, so as to experience equality, liberty and fraternity in the society today. Along with Varna system he urges to do away with the Caste system too. In the following pages I will try to explain Ambedkar's thoughts on Casteism.

2.2. Elimination of the Caste System

In Ambedkar's opinion unless there is change in the existing social order people can achieve very little by way of progress. Anything that is based on the foundation of Caste, he says, will crack and will never be a whole. He therefore considers 'the abolishment of Caste' as of prime importance. But the problem of the ways and means for abolishing the Caste system is a difficult and complicated one. Ambedkar here critically examines the various ways suggested by the reformers in the past for the reform of the Hindu social order. Later he proposes a new way of reform which he hopes will solve the problem.

Some reformers are of the view that in the reform of Caste, the first step to take is 'to abolish the sub-Caste'. It is based on the supposition that there is a greater similarity in manners and status between sub-Castes than there is between Castes. Ambedkar sees this supposition as erroneous as the different sub-Castes are not at par with one another, in the different parts of the country. Further he asks: "What guarantee is there that the abolition of the sub-Castes will necessarily lead to the abolition of Caste? On the contrary the abolition will only help to strengthen the big Castes, make them powerful and therefore more tyrannical and oppressive."[121] Ambedkar therefore regards this remedy as ineffective and impractical.

[121] Ambedkar, "Annihilation of Caste" 67.

Another plan of action suggested for abolition of Caste is to begin with 'inter-Caste dinners'. Ambedkar regards this too as inadequate. He remarks that though there are many Castes who allow inter-dining, it is our common experience that inter-dining has not succeeded in killing the spirit of Caste and the consciousness of Caste.[122]

According to Ambedkar the real remedy for the abolition of Caste is 'inter-marriage'. He is fully convinced that this 'fusion of blood' can alone create the feeling of kinship and of being kindred, if not the feeling of being aliens created by Caste will not vanish. The practice of inter-marriage will automatically include the inter-dining in it. Ambedkar therefore concludes that Caste will cease to be an operative force only, when 'inter-marriage and inter-dining have become matters of common concern.'[123]

However, Ambedkar observes, large majority of Hindu are opposed to these practices because inter-dining and inter-marriages are repugnant to the beliefs and dogmas which they regard as sacred and divine. Castes, he says, are not a physical barrier like a wall, which prevents the co-mingling of Hindus. Basically it is a notion, a state of mind. The destruction of Caste therefore means a national change. Further, he stresses, we must realize that the Hindus observe Caste with all its evils, not because they are inhuman or wrongheaded but because they are deeply religious. It is not the people who observe Caste who are wrong, but their religion or Shastras which has inculcated in them the notion of Caste. The real remedy for intermarriages to be possible, he thinks, is to destroy the belief in the sanctity of the Shastras for the acts of the people are merely the result of their beliefs, inculcated in their minds by the Shastras. People will not change their conduct, until they cease to believe in the sanctity of the Shastras on which their conduct is founded.[124]

Thus, for Ambedkar, to agitate for and to organize inter-Caste dinners and inter-Caste marriages is like forced feeding brought about by artificial means. Only when people are free from deep

[122] Ambedkar, "Annihilation of Caste" 67.

[123] Ambedkar, "Annihilation of Caste" 67-68.

[124] Ambedkar, "Annihilation of Caste" 68.

rooted religious prejudices or sacred notions behind Castes, he says, will they inter-dine and inter-marry on a mass scale without any fear of divine wrath.[125]

From the standpoint of reason and morality, Ambedkar observes, the destruction of the feeling and notion of sanctity and divinity behind the Caste is essential, as reason and morality appear to have no place in Hindu Shastras. Any new change once well established denies reason and morality. The sacredness of Hindu social organization is well established and Caste has acquired a divine basis. Therefore, if a new social order, based on reason and morality is to be brought about, then the divinity behind the Caste, i.e., behind the Shastras, Ambedkar stresses, should be destroyed.[126]

While speaking about religion Ambedkar makes clear the distinction between rule and principle. According to him rules are practical while the principles are intellectual. Here he remarks:

> Doing what is said to be by virtue of a rule and doing good in the light of a principle are two different things. The principle may be wrong but the act is conscious and responsible. The rule may be right but the act is mechanical. A religious act may not be a correct act but must at least be a responsible act. ...The moment it degenerates into rules it ceases to be religion, as it kills responsibility which is the essence of a truly religious act.[127]

Further, Ambedkar says, more than a set of principles, Hindu religion is a 'code of rules' because it contains nothing but a mass of sacrificial, social political and sanitary rules and regulations, all mixed up. It is a multitude of commands and prohibitions which can be termed as 'legalized class-ethics'. Moreover, the iniquities they perpetuate seem to be the same for all generations. He therefore refuses to call this code of ordinances as religion and calls people for

---

[125] Ambedkar, "Annihilation of Caste" 68-69.

[126] Ambedkar, "Annihilation of Caste" 72-75.

[127] Ambedkar, "Annihilation of Caste" 75.

the destruction of such an irreligious religion so as to bring about a social change in the society.[128]

Although he condemns the 'religion of rules' he does not hold that there is no necessity for a religion. On the contrary, he agrees with Burke when he says that, "True religion is the foundation of society, the basis on which all true Civil Government rests, and both their sanction". Consequently, when he urges that these ancient rules of life be annulled, he is anxious to see its place be taken by a 'Religion of Principles', which alone can lay claim to being a true religion.[129]

Ambedkar thus suggests reform of the religion by giving it a new basis based on Liberty, Equality and Fraternity; in short, Democracy. This new basis of modern society, he hopes, will help in killing the spirit of Caste consciousness and exclusiveness. It means a complete change in the fundamental notion of life, in the values of life, and in outlook and attitude towards human beings and things.[130] Indeed, "the old must cease to be operative before the new can begin to enliven and to pulsate". This is what he means, when he says: "The people must discard the authority of the Shastras and destroy the religion of the Shastras."[131]

Thus Ambedkar believes that the Caste order can be eliminated only if the sense of divinity and sacredness behind it is rejected. Only then, can inter-dining and inter-marriage be effective in bringing about a national change in Caste. Only then the people will get rid of all their inequalities and learn to enjoy the social freedom.

2.3. The Liberation of Women

Ambedkar was not only bothered about the discrimination of Caste but he was sensitive to other injustices as well. While speaking about the eradication of the social evils he points out to the treatment given to the women and the life of a slave that they had to live in his time. Here, he brings to our notice how the laws of Manu degraded the

---

[128] Ambedkar, "Annihilation of Caste" 76.

[129] Ambedkar, "Annihilation of Caste" 76.

[130] Ambedkar, "Annihilation of Caste" 77-78.

[131] Ambedkar, "Annihilation of Caste" 78.

Hindu women and fights back for the emancipation of women in the wake of creating an ideal social order.

As Ambedkar observes, Manu can hardly be said to be tenderer to women than he was to the Shudra. In fact he has a very low opinion of women. In Manu's own words:

> II. 213. It is the nature of women to seduce men in this (world), for that reason the wise are never unguarded in (the company of) females.
>
> II. 214. For women are able to lead astray in (this) world not only a fool, but even a learned man, and (to make) him a slave of desire and anger.
>
> IX. 14. Women do not care for beauty, nor is their attention fixed in age (thinking); '(It is enough that) he is a man', they give themselves to the handsome and to the ugly.
>
> IX. 15. Through their passion for men, through their mutable temper, through their natural heartlessness, they become disloyal towards their husbands, however, carefully they may be guarded in this (world).[132]

Because of all these ideas that Manu carried in his mind, he did not want women to be free under any circumstances. In his opinion:

> IX. 2. Day and night women must be kept in dependence by the males (of their families), and, if they attach themselves to sexual enjoyments, they must be kept under one's control.
>
> V. 149. She must not seek to separate herself from her father, husband, or sons, as by leaving them she would make both (her own and her husband's) families contemptible. Woman is not to have a right to divorce.[133]

---

[132] B.R. Ambedkar, "The Woman and the Counter-Revolution" *Writings and Speeches – Vol. 3* (Bombay: The Education Department - Government of Maharashtra, 1987), 429.

[133] Ambedkar, "The Woman and the Counter-Revolution" 430.

Many people, after knowing Manu's law of divorce, are of the view that Manu regarded marriage as a sacrament and therefore, did not allow divorce. This is far from truth, as Ambedkar observes, his law of divorce had a different motive. It was not to tie up a man to a woman but it was to tie up the woman to a man and to leave the man free.[134]

Manu does not prevent a man from giving up his wife. Indeed he not only allows him to abandon his wife but also permits him to sell her. What he does is to prevent the wife from becoming free. This is because he wanted to deprive woman of the freedom she had under the Buddhist regime. He knew that by the misuse of her liberty, by her willingness to marry the Shudra the system of the gradation of the Varna had been destroyed. Manu was outraged by her licence and in putting a stop to it he deprived her of her liberty. Even in the matter of property a wife was reduced by Manu to the level of a slave. (IX 416).[135] A woman under his law was subjected to corporal punishment and Manu allows the husband, the right to beat his wife (VIII 299). The study of the Veda too was forbidden to her by him as it was to the Shudra (II 66, IX 18).[136]

Offering sacrifices according to Brahmanism formed the very soul of religion yet Manu did not allow a woman to perform them. Further to discourage her from performing such sacrifices Manu prevented her from getting the aid and services of a Brahmin priest.[137] In short, women, in Manu's time, were not to have any intellectual pursuits or free will, nor freedom of thought, which degraded them to the rank of a slave.

This was not so, as Ambedkar observes, in the pre-Manu period where a woman was entitled to Upanayana ceremony. This is clear from the Atharva Veda where a girl is spoken of as a being eligible for marriage having finished her Brahmacharya. From, the Sharauta sutras it is clear that the women could repeat the mantras

---

[134] Ambedkar, "The Woman and the Counter-Revolution" 430.

[135] The numbers in the bracket correspond to the laws of Manu as quoted by Ambedkar in his third volume.

[136] Ambedkar, "The Woman and the Counter-Revolution" 430-431.

[137] Ambedkar, "The Woman and the Counter-Revolution" 431.

of the Vedas and they were even taught to read the Vedas. Panini's Ashtaadhyai bears testimony to the fact that women attended Gurukul and studied the various Shakhas of the Veda and became expert in Mimamsa. Patanjali's Maha Bhasya shows that women were teachers and taught Vedas to girl students. There are many stories of women entering into public discussions with men on most abstruse subjects of Religion, Philosophy and Metaphysics. This goes to show that Indian women, in pre-Manu's time, could rise to the highest pinnacle of learning and education.[138] Thus, the fact that women in pre-Manu days were highly respected cannot be disputed.

According to Ambedkar, unlike Manu in Kautilya's[139] time, women could claim divorce on the ground of mutual enmity and hatred. A wife was allowed to abandon her husband if he was of a bad character. There was no ban on a woman or a widow remarrying and if she desired she could begin to live independently. Unlike Manu every precaution was taken to guarantee economic independence to a married woman, in fact in Kautilya's time a wife could even bring an action in a court of law against her husband for assault and defamation.[140] In short in pre-Manu days a woman was free and was treated as equal to a man.

Ambedkar wanted to give the women of today the same status as they had in Kautilya's time or in the pre-Manu period. He wanted to create equal rights for both a man and a woman. He realized the discrimination created by Manu with regard to the social status of Hindu religion. He therefore strives to liberate the Hindu women from their slavery created by Manu's laws and to give them freedom of thought and movement, and right to education.

Ambedkar, being the great believer in women's progress and organization, was aware of the united strength of women towards the improvement of the society. He therefore calls them to come together to fight for their common purposes and thus to bring about social reform in the society.[141] He was happy that women in India

---

[138] Ambedkar, "The Woman and the Counter-Revolution" 432.

[139] Kautilya = the author of Arthashastra.

[140] Ambedkar, "The Woman and the Counter-Revolution" 434.

[141] Ambedkar, "The Woman and the Counter-Revolution" 434-436.

have achieved a sense of human dignity and have made progress in all spheres of their life. Dhananjay Keer summarizes the advice of Ambedkar to women, with a deep faith in their emancipation, as follows:

(i) Learn to be clean.
(ii) Keep away from vices.
(iii) Give education to your children.
(iv) Remove from yourselves all inferiority complexes.
(v) Instill ambition into yourselves.
(vi) Inculcate in your minds that you are destined to be great.[142]

Ambedkar holds that marriage is a liability. Parents should not impose it upon their children unless they are financially able to meet the liabilities arising from marriage.[143] He was against the social evils created by the early marriage system in Indian society. In particular, he was mainly opposed to the social customs of sati, enforced widowhood and girl (child) marriage.[144]

Ambedkar's advice to the marriageable girls could be summarized in the following words:

> Do not be in a hurry to marry.... Those who will marry will have to keep in mind that to have too many children is a crime. The parental duty lies in giving each child a better start than its parents had. Above all, let every girl who marries stand by her husband, claim to be her husbands' friend and equal, and refuse to be his slave. I am sure if you follow this advice, you will bring honor and glory to yourselves.[145]

Ambedkar wants to make not only men but also women bold and fearless, courageous and intelligent, so that they can manage many

---

[142] Dhananjay Keer, *Dr. Ambedkar: Life and Mission* (Bombay: Popular Prakashan, 1954), 352.

[143] D.R. Jatava, *The Political Philosophy of B.R. Ambedkar* (Agra: Phoenix Publication House, 1965), 27.

[144] Ambedkar, "Castes in India" 13.

[145] Keer, *Dr. Ambedkar: Life and Mission*, 352.

of their affairs themselves in their homes and in their communities. He says: "Never regard yourselves as Untouchables. Live a clean life. Dress yourself like the touchable ladies, never mind if your dress is full of patches, but see that it is clean. None can restrict your freedom in the choice of your garments and in the use of the metal for your ornaments. Attend more to the cultivation of the mind and the spirit of self-help."[146] All these personal and human rights were denied to the women of Untouchable communities in Hindu society. Therefore, Ambedkar's was a just cause to rouse the consciousness of these women against inhuman restrictions imposed upon them.

He stresses the need for the cultivation of the mind and the spirit of self-help among the men and the women. He wants them to realize that they owe a great responsibility for educating their children in the right way. To him, education is the most important factor for moulding the life of all men, women and children. He observes: "Education is as necessary for females as it is for males. If you know how to read and write, there would be much progress. As you are, so your children will be. Mould their lives in virtuous ways, for sons should be such as would make a mark in this world."[147]

Thus, Ambedkar who was the symbol and hope of the suppressed people, smashed the walls of bondage, tyranny and exploitation to free women from their social degradation and uplift them on the level of social and political equality. Like all men, he wanted the women too, to contribute to the good of the society and nation and to shun what hampers their freedom, growth and prosperity. Thus, all his efforts for the emancipation of women were geared towards bringing them on par with men, enabling them to share equal responsibility with men in human progress and advancement of humanity.

---

[146] Keer, *Dr. Ambedkar: Life and Mission*, 104.

[147] Keer, *Dr. Ambedkar: Life and Mission*, 104.

Chapter 4

Emancipation through Conversion

Ambedkar, along with his five lakh Dalit brethren, renounced Hinduism and embraced Buddhism on 14th October, 1956 at Nagpur. His decision for religious conversion created uproar among the Caste Hindus and as a consequence, he, along with his people, had to face a lot of opposition and criticism. This historical event gives rise to many questions such as - why did Ambedkar choose a religious solution to the problems of the Untouchables? Why did he reject all other religions and opt for Buddhism? How far is the conversion movement successful in elevating the Untouchables-socially, economically and politically? What dent did he make on Untouchability by embracing Buddhism? This chapter addresses itself to all these questions.

1. Religious Conversion as a means of Liberation

In order to discard his ancient religion which stood for inequality and oppression, Ambedkar chose to go for religious conversion. His religious conversion was a revolt against the suppression and enslavement of humanity. While making his stand clear on conversion he says that it is impossible to get liberation of Untouchables by remaining within Hinduism. Since 'Hinduism' is the other name for the Caste system on which it is built, he says, Untouchability will go on as long as the Caste system is there. Therefore, it is not possible for the Dalits to get equality by remaining as Hindus.[148]

While clarifying his views with regard to the aim of conversion, he says:

> To Reform the Hindu Society is neither our aim nor our field of action. Our aim is to gain freedom. …if we can gain our freedom by conversion, why should we shoulder the responsibility of reforming the Hindu religion? … None should misunderstand the object of our movement as being Hindu social reform. The object of our movement is to achieve social freedom for the Untouchables. It is equally true that this freedom cannot be secured without conversion.[149]

He thus makes it clear that what the Dalits are interested in is not reform but revolution to save themselves. The only way for their freedom, he suggests, is through conversion.

According to Ambedkar, this conversion of religion will bring happiness to both the Untouchables as well as the Hindus. For as long as the Untouchables remain Hindus, they will have to struggle for social intercourse, for food and water, and for inter-Caste marriages. By conversion, the roots of all their quarrels will vanish. Thus through conversion, Ambedkar observes, the equality of treatment can be achieved and the affinity between the Hindus and the Untouchables can be brought about. Ambedkar therefore sees the path of conversion as the only right path of freedom which ultimately leads to equality.[150]

Ambedkar stood not only for religious conversion but also for the conversion of human personality. He wanted all men - poor

---

[148] B.R. Ambedkar, "Philosophy of Hinduism" *Writings and Speeches – Vol. 3* (Bombay: The Education Department - Government of Maharashtra, 1987), 5-6.

[149] Ambedkar, "Philosophy of Hinduism" 5.

[150] Ambedkar, "Philosophy of Hinduism" 19.

and proletariat - to pass from a lower (empirical) plane to a higher (rational) plane of human living, because the old set of values was completely inoperative and harmful to all men and women. In his religious conversion, the first characteristic is that the set of values should be determined through rational consciousness which claimed supreme validity for itself.[151]

Ambedkar, as an Untouchable, experienced all the moments of material suffering and intellectual agony. The life of an Untouchable which he wanted to be converted from was not worth living. After careful and deep thought, he visualized that religious conversion was essential to rouse the rational consciousness of man against religious hypocrisy and dishonesty. According to him his religious conversion was not inspired by any material motive but it was mainly the spiritual feeling that was underlying his religious conversion.[152]

One may ask, what exactly inspired Ambedkar to effect such a radical transformation of human personality and social set-up? As we have understood him, he had an idea of the higher life and he wanted to realize it. There is no doubt that religious conversion requires any human being to sacrifice all that is traditionally attached to him. Even then there is no guarantee that the new mode of life can be successfully realized. This sort of conversion is not possible unless there is a strong mind and clear thinking in the person who wants it. Ambedkar was prepared to meet all such risks and social opposition with immense courage.[153]

Ambedkar's approach to conversion was purely humanistic and as a humanist, he expressed the spirit of humanism in his act of religious conversion. He had faith in a human being's potentialities. He always felt closer to the poor, the weak and the hopeless. He wished all to be benefited by faith, love and knowledge. His religious conversion was, in reality a factual and rational assessment of those human values which are most useful to human being's immediate needs and intellectual curiosity. His act of religious conversion was

---

[151] Jatava, *The Social Philosophy of B.R. Ambedkar*, 34.

[152] Jatava, *The Social Philosophy of B.R. Ambedkar*, 34.

[153] Jatava, *The Social Philosophy of B.R. Ambedkar*, 34-35.

thus essentially social. To sum up, according to Dr. D. R. Jatava, this heroic decision of Ambedkar involves:

1. The rational consciousness of assessing things for a better life of human beings;
2. The freedom of choice in which man realizes his individual dignity;
3. The realization of the higher life by transcending the lower plane of human existence;
4. The revolt against the suppression and enslavement of humanity;
5. The entire change of traditional pattern of society for providing physical facilities for all;
6. The emancipation of ignored humanity and the revitalization of overlooked reality.[154]

2. Ambedkar's Rejection of Dalit's Conversion to Christianity

Ambedkar here makes an attempt to examine critically the condition of those Untouchables who have been already converted to Christianity, with the help of suitable examples. This gives us the reason as to why he was not in favor of Dalits being converted to Christianity. According to him, although the work and efforts put in by the Christian missionaries in the field of education and medical aid are notable and praiseworthy, still many questions remain to be answered in this respect. Such as - What has Christianity achieved in the way of changing mentality of the converts? Has the Untouchable convert risen to the status of the Touchable? Have the Touchable and Untouchables converts discarded Caste? Have they ceased to worship their old pagan gods and to adhere to their old pagan superstitions? He poses all these questions to all the Christians in India and he wants the 'Christianity in India' to stand or fall by the answers it can give to these questions.[155]

---

[154] Jatava, *The Social Philosophy of B.R. Ambedkar*, 38.

[155] B.R. Ambedkar, "The Condition of the Convert" *Writings and Speeches – Vol. 5* (Bombay: The Education Department - Government of Maharashtra, 1989), 454.

Ambedkar here quotes the following extract taken from the memorandum submitted by the Christian depressed classes of South India to the Simon Commission which throws light on the position of the Untouchables who have gone into the Christian fold so far as the question of Caste is concerned.

> We are by religion Christians, both Roman Catholics and Protestants. Of the total population of Indian Christians of the Presidency the converts from the Depressed Classes form about sixty percent. When the Christian religion was preached on our lands, we, the Pallas, Pariahs, Malas, Madiga, etc., embraced Christianity. But others of our stock and origin were not converted and they are known to be the Hindu Depressed classes, being all Hindus or adherents to the Hindus in religion. In spite, however, of our Christian religion which teaches us fundamental truths about the equality of man and man before God, the necessity of charity and love for neighbors and mutual sympathy and forbearance, we the large number of the Depressed classes converts remain in the same social condition as the Hindu Depressed classes. Through the operation of several factors, the more important of them being the strong Caste retaining Hindu mentality of the converts to Christianity, and the indifference, powerlessness and apathy of the Missionaries, we remain today what we were before we became Christians – Untouchables - degraded by the laws of social position obtaining in the land, rejected Caste Christians, despised by Caste Hindus and excluded by our own Hindu Depressed Class brethren.[156]

In support of this report, Ambedkar gives us the example of the 'Caste Christians' in Madras. Although the term 'Caste Christians' sounds a contradiction, Ambedkar observes that in Madras it is the correct and accepted description of high Caste converts from Hinduism, who retain all the rigor and exclusiveness of Caste. The Untouchable converts are therefore treated by them as Untouchables

156 Ambedkar, "The Condition of the Convert" 454.

and unapproachable even in the Churches, denying the very foundations of Christianity, i.e., love, charity and brotherhood. He thus remarks that the Depressed class Christians are treated by the 'fellow-Christians' in the same way as Hindu Depressed classes are treated by the Hindu Caste people.[157]

Another fact that Ambedkar notices among the convert Christians is that they still retain the Hindu form of worship and believe in Hindu superstition. According to him, Christianity has not been effective in wiping paganism out of converts because although the Christian Missionaries were eager to convert persons to Christianity, they never put up a determined fight to uproot paganism from the convert. In fact, he says, they tolerated it.[158] That is the reason why today the religious observances, which are incompatible with Christian belief and Christian way of life, are still being practiced by the Christian converts.

The Christian Missionaries, Ambedkar observes, initially found it very difficult to continue their work of conversion due to the existing Caste system. The Missionaries therefore agreed that Christianity should be made easy in order that it may spread in India. They therefore tolerated the inequalities of Castes on the ground that it was an ingrained part of Hindu religion. In adopting this policy, he remarks the Missionaries never thought that some day somebody would ask them, 'what good is Christianity for a Hindu if it does not do away with his Caste? According to him they misunderstood their mission and thought that making a person Christian was the same thing as making him a follower of Christ.[159]

Ambedkar remarks that the Untouchables remain Untouchables to the general mass of Hindus even though they have become Christians. An Untouchable even after his conversion to Christianity has to face the same ill-treatment at the hands of Caste Hindus as he would get before conversion. He therefore raises the question: "Why has Christianity not succeeded in raising the status of the

---

[157] Ambedkar, "The Condition of the Convert" 454-455.

[158] Ambedkar, "The Condition of the Convert" 456.

[159] Ambedkar, "The Condition of the Convert" 466-470.

Untouchables convert?"[160] Here, he tries to come up with some reasons which touch the very roots of this problem.

As Ambedkar analyses this problem further he realizes that a change in the social status of the convert can be the result of a two-field change. i) There must be a change in the attitude of the Hindus. ii) There must be a change in the attitude of the converts.

While considering the first part, Ambedkar replies that Christianity has done nothing to make the Hindus move on. The dependence of those in charge of Christian religion upon planting of an idea and leaving it to work a miracle, he says, is the important reason as to why the Untouchable has remained an Untouchable notwithstanding his Christian faith.[161] While looking at the second part, Ambedkar realizes that Christianity itself does not inspire the convert to move on. He finds that more than the 'practical reforms' of the converts, Christian preaching is mostly centered around their 'spiritual development'. He also hints at the lack of interest on the part of the Christian Missionaries to act and remove the injustice which pursues the Untouchables even after their conversion to Christianity.[162]

Ultimately, Ambedkar gives two reasons as to why Christian Untouchables have failed to raise a movement against the social injustice done to them: i) The complete absence of desire on the part of the educated among the Christians (mostly the high Caste Christians), to take up the cause of the community and fight for it, which leaves the Untouchable Christians totally leaderless to fight for their rights. ii) The faults in the mental make-up of the convert which is characterized by a complete absence of any urge to break his bounds.[163]

This again, Ambedkar says, is due to two reasons: i) An Untouchable becomes a Christian for some advantage or because he likes the teaching of the Bible. But very rarely it is because of his discontentment of the Hindu religious teachings. This results

[160] Ambedkar, "The Condition of the Convert" 470.

[161] Ambedkar, "The Condition of the Convert" 470-471.

[162] Ambedkar, "The Condition of the Convert" 470.

[163] Ambedkar, "The Condition of the Convert" 472.

in Christianity becoming addendum to his old faith instead of substituting his old faith. He thus ends up in observing both the religious appropriately. ii) Instead of teaching the Untouchable that his fall is due to wrong social or religious environment, which he must attack to improve his condition, he is told to accept his fall as due to original sin. This teaching does not distinguish the convert from a Hindu who believes that his fall is due to karma and keeps him passive towards the social injustice done to him.[164]

Ambedkar observes the fact that in India today the Indian Christian community is not really counted while the other minorities such as Muslims and Sikhs are well recognized by the Indian Government. He comes up with two factors as to account for this situation: i) A large majority of Indian Christians are totally dependent upon the missionaries for their education, medical care, religious ministration, etc. Since they do not depend upon Government, they do not care to agitate, educate or organize their masses for effective political action. Since they are without any organization the Government too does not care to attend to their needs and requirements which results in they not having a recognized place in public. ii) Secondly, the 'Indian Christian' is a disjointed community. Like all other Indians they too have been divided by race, language and Caste. Their religion has not been a sufficiently strong unifying force to supersede these distinctions. The result is that the Indian Christians are too disjointed to have a common aim and common mind, and to come together for a common endeavor.[165]

Thus through the exploration of the lives of the Christian Dalit converts, Ambedkar gives us full account of their problems. He tries to bring to our notice the ill-treatment they have to suffer and the inhuman conditions in which they have to live even after being converted to Christianity. He thus makes us aware of the fact that the conversion of the Untouchables to Christianity has made very little difference to the social status of the converts.

---

[164] Ambedkar, "The Condition of the Convert" 472-73.

[165] Ambedkar, "The Condition of the Convert" 473-476.

3. Option for Buddhism

While expressing his opinion about his conversion to Buddhism, Ambedkar says:

> By discarding my ancient religion which stood for inequality and oppression today I am reborn. I have no faith in the philosophy of incarnation; and it is wrong and mischievous to say that Buddha was an incarnation of Vishnu. I am no more a devotee of any Hindu god or goddess. I will not perform Shraddha. I will strictly follow the eightfold path of Buddha. Buddhism is a true religion and I will lead a life guided by the three principles of knowledge, right path and compassion.[166]

Thus the realization of a good life combined with knowledge and guided by the spirit of love and equality was the main aim behind Ambedkar's conversion to Buddhism. It was not merely an individual act, but also a social event for the emancipation of ignored section of humanity and the revitalization of overlooked reality.

Ambedkar's conversion to Buddhism was not revenge, nor was it against the tradition of this country. As he says: "Buddhism is a part and parcel of Bharatiya culture. I have taken care that my conversion will not harm the tradition of the culture and history of this land."[167] His conversion to Buddhism was an effort to reach humanity and to enrich the life of the common person. It was a message of new life for those who yearned for human dignity. Ambedkar also stresses on the freedom of choice as every person has either to choose the higher plane of values or to keep oneself to the lower plane. He identified himself with the idea of religious conversion in order to realize the higher plane of human life. This way of life enlightened him to rouse millions of men and women from dogmatism, superstition and ignorance. Jatava quotes him thus: "I prefer Buddhism, because it gives three principles in combination, which no other religion does. Buddhism teaches prajna (understanding as against superstition and

---

[166] Keer, *Dr. Ambedkar: Life and Mission*, 497.

[167] Keer, *Dr. Ambedkar: Life and Mission*, 495.

supernaturalism, karuna (love), and samata (equality). This is what man wants for a good and happy life."[168]

Thus, according to Ambedkar, the essentials of religion – morality, reason, liberty, equality, fraternity, etc. – that he wants in a true religion are present in Buddha's religion. He therefore regards Buddha's Dhamma as true religion, the purpose of which is to reconstruct the world by establishing right relations among human beings.[169]

---

[168] Jatava, *The Social Philosophy of B.R. Ambedkar*, 37.

[169] Jatava, *The Political Philosophy of B.R. Ambedkar*, 36.

Chapter 5

Towards a New Social Order

Ambedkar rejects the traditional Hindu social order because of its denial of the ideals of social humanism, viz., liberty and equality, to the people belonging to Scheduled Castes. He therefore sought to create a new social order based on the principles of social humanism, viz., liberty, equality and fraternity. This type of social order, for Ambedkar, would destroy the prevalent Caste system, give equal rights and privileges to all human beings, and thus bring about the social upliftment of the Shudras and the Untouchables, the so-called Scheduled Caste people.

In his proposed new social order, Ambedkar stresses on an ideal social organization based on the principles of liberty, equality and fraternity, the democratic way of life, the concepts of state socialism and common good, and the non-violent method of social change. In the present chapter I will briefly explain each one of them so as to grasp and understand Ambedkar's vision of the new social order.

1. An Ideal Social Organization

Ambedkar is vehemently opposed to the wrong ideals of the Hindu society. As already seen in the previous chapters, he condemns the social order which is based on Varnas and Castes. He is therefore striving for an ideal society, which will be free of all these social evils. However to him, an ideal society is a different one. "If you ask me", he says, "My ideal would be a society based on Liberty, Equality and Fraternity."[170]

These three words are of greatest importance in Ambedkar's social philosophy and they are not derived from the slogan of the French revolution but from the teaching of Buddha. He reiterates: "Positively, my social philosophy may be said to be enshrined in three words: liberty equality and fraternity. Let no one however say that I have borrowed my philosophy from the French Revolution. I have not. My philosophy has roots in religion and not in political science. I have derived them from my master Buddha."[171] Let us now proceed further to understand the ideals of liberty, equality and fraternity which are the cornerstones of Ambedkar's concept of 'ideal society'.

1.1. Liberty

In Indian society according to Ambedkar, a measure of liberty is essential and necessary to create and maintain a free democratic social order. In his concept of social order he does not oppose the right to private property but demands liberty in the sense of a right to property, tools and materials as being necessary for earning a living to keep the body in due state of health. This principle can only be maintained, if a person has the right to acquire his or her living by his/her own 'choice', which will allow them for independent enterprise leading to a greater efficiency in the working of socio-economic machine.[172]

To object to an individual's freedom 'to choose one's own profession', Ambedkar argues, is to perpetuate slavery by compelling the individuals to carry on certain prescribed callings which are not of their choice. Respect for the free will of every individual is, then,

---

[170] Ambedkar, "Annihilation of Caste" 57.

[171] Keer, *Dr. Ambedkar: Life and Mission*, 456.

[172] Jatava, *The Social Philosophy of B.R. Ambedkar*, 86-87.

the corner stone of Ambedkar's social order, for self-determination is the essence of human existence.[173]

Being a staunch supporter of the liberty of thought and expression Ambedkar is totally in favour of a parliamentary or representative government, which, he thinks will secure a government based on law, with a minimum of social and economic injustice. Thus in the interest of political liberty, Ambedkar allows a place for parliamentary government as the best form of government, both in the interests of the individual and the society.[174]

Religious freedom too has an important place in his ideal society as he wants every individual to be free to choose his own religion. According to him, all human beings, who adhere to some particular religions, should have rights to form religious associations on the basis of which they can lead their lives.[175] He also wants the state to guarantee to its entire citizenry "the liberty of conscience and the free exercise of their religion including the right to profess, to preach and to convert within limits compatible with public order and morality."[176] He thus stands for individual's religious freedom for intellectual and spiritual enlightenment.

Thus, although the ideal of liberty as conceived by Ambedkar emphasizes on 'the pursuing of one's profession by one's own choice' as the essence of individual liberty, it also stands for all kind of liberty – social, political and religious.

1.2. Equality

The term 'Equality' is more often prescriptive than descriptive when used in social and political theories. Taken, in this sense, 'all humans are equal' would imply not that they actually possess attributes in the same degree; but that "they ought to be treated alike."[177] Ambedkar

[173] Jatava, *The Social Philosophy of B.R. Ambedkar*, 87.

[174] Jatava, *The Social Philosophy of B.R. Ambedkar*, 87-88.

[175] B.R. Ambedkar, *States and Minorities* (Bombay: Sindhu Publication Private Limited, 1947), 11-12.

[176] Ambedkar, *States and Minorities*, 11.

[177] S.I. Benn and R.S. Peters, *Social Principles and the Democratic State* (London: Allen & Unwin, 1959) as cited in D.R. Jatava, *The Social Philosophy of B.R. Ambedkar* (Agra: Phoenix Publication House, 1965), 108.

is very much of the same view. "The objection to equality" he says, "may be sound and one must have to admit that all men are not equal. But what of that? Equality may be a fiction, but nonetheless one must accept it as the governing principle."[178]

Ambedkar observes that a person's power is dependent upon i) physical heredity, ii) social inheritance or endowment in the form of parental care, education, accumulation of scientific knowledge, etc., and iii) on his own efforts. He admits that human beings are 'unequal' in all these three aspects.[179] If, therefore, a selection is made, owing to the first two types of inequalities, it will not necessarily be selection of 'the able and the fit'; rather it will be the selection of the 'privileged'. Obviously, such selection will be contrary to the spirit of social democracy – the principle of social humanism. The reason, therefore, which forces that in the third aspect (in individual effects) we should treat people unequally, demands that in the first two aspects (physical heredity and social inheritance) we should treat people as equally as possible.[180]

Ambedkar, therefore, in his ideal of equality, lays emphasis on the ideal of 'equality of consideration'. "Equality of consideration means that none shall be held to have a claim to better treatment than another, in advance of good grounds produced."[181] This includes impartiality and justice as well as the consideration of the legitimate demands of the poorer section of society. Ambedkar's argument for the 'equality of consideration' is mainly because of the 'inequality of opportunity' that the servile classes have suffered at the hands of Caste Hindus.[182]

According to Ambedkar, every statesman, from the political point of view, is bound to recognize this demand for equality as the governing principle of life. Since the classification and assortment of

---

[178] Ambedkar, "Annihilation of Caste" 39.

[179] Ambedkar, "Annihilation of Caste" 39.

[180] Ambedkar, "Annihilation of Caste" 39-40.

[181] S.I. Benn and R.S. Peters, *Social Principles and the Democratic State* (London: Allen & Unwin, 1959) as cited in D.R. Jatava, *The Social Philosophy of B.R. Ambedkar*, 110.

[182] B.R. Ambedkar, *Pakistan or the Partition of India* (Bombay: Thacker and Co. Ltd, 1946), 137.

a vast number of people is impossible, the politicians, he emphasizes, must at least follow some 'rough and ready' rule to treat all people alike, not because they are alike, but because their classification and assortment is impossible.[183]

Ambedkar thus stresses that people ought to be given equal chances to develop and grow though it which is not the same as identity of opportunity. Thus, in his concept of social equality, he asks for 'equality of consideration' and 'equality of opportunity', which he thinks, will enable all the people to participate in an effective social organization.

1.3. Fraternity

Generally, the meaning of principle of fraternity is taken as 'charity', but Ambedkar's idea of fraternity differs from this traditional view. According to him,

> An ideal society should be mobile, should be full of channels for conveying a change, taking place in one part to other parts. In our ideal society, there should be many interests consciously communicated and shared. There should be varied and free points of contact with other modes of association - in short, there must be social endosmosis.[184]

On the basis of this he wishes to erect the tower of social democracy. Fraternity for him is only another name for democracy and he does not limit democracy to mere form of government. For him, it is a mode of associated living, of combined communicated experience. He considers it, essentially, as an attitude of respect and reverence towards fellowmen.[185] Thus, 'fraternity' as the third principle of his ideal society which insists upon spirit of service, love, brotherhood, and communication is geared towards the avoidance of class-hatred, class-warfare, revengefulness and the like.

Ambedkar's view of society thus includes freedom, equality and fraternity. Here he emerges as a staunch supporter of social democracy,

---

[183] Ambedkar, "Annihilation of Caste" 38.

[184] Ambedkar, "Annihilation of Caste" 38.

[185] Ambedkar, "Annihilation of Caste" 38.

of an ideal society, of society without Caste system. According to him, this democratic society should not merely be a matter of dogma but must be realistic so that it could be made the possession of all and not the privilege of a few.[186] Only then a true spirit of fraternal relationship may be strengthened among people. His ideal social organization aims at just and equitable relations between one person and another based on choice, equal consideration, equal opportunity and brotherly love.

Thus, his vision of an ideal social organization is based on the fundamental principles of liberty, equality and fraternity. The society, so formed, shall be a welfare society in order:

(i) to secure the blessings of both, of self-government and good government;
(ii) to maintain the right of every individual to life, liberty and pursuit of happiness and to free speech and the exercise of religion;
(iii) to remove social, political and economic inequalities by providing better opportunities to all masses in society;
(iv) to make it possible for every individual to enjoy freedom from want and freedom from fear; and
(v) to provide against internal disorder, injustice, tyranny and oppression.[187]

In the next section we will see as to why Ambedkar treats the concept of common good as a necessity in an 'ideal social organization'.

2. The Concept of Common Good

The concept of common good, in Ambedkar's socio-political thought, is of prime importance as common good is considered by him to be an important aim of human life. Throughout his life he remained a staunch advocate of a society formed and maintained for the betterment of the condition of the poor, the fallen and the weak.

As Ambedkar observes, the organization of Indian society since medieval times has caused many ills in the socio- political life. People

---

[186] Ambedkar, *Pakistan or the Partition of India*, 208.

[187] Jatava, *The Social Philosophy of B.R. Ambedkar*, 93.

have suffered from social stagnation, communal aggression and national frustration.[188] Ambedkar holds out the hopes of a better future - a society based on the principles of liberty, equality and fraternity, self- respect and self- help.[189] According to him a society without social equality, freedom and brotherhood cannot achieve the real aim of its revolution, however successful it may be in other respects.[190] What he strives for is a socialistic society based on human friendship, love and goodwill between one person and another, which will also at the same time retain the freedom of the individual.

For establishing socialism, Ambedkar does not feel the necessity of under-rating the importance and status of the individual, nor does he believe in the increased use of force as in society. He emphatically differs from both the Marxists and the Socialists, who think that harmony can be reached only through totalitarianism. Therefore, according to him, to allow one class to impose restrictions on another in matters of earning a livelihood or performing a religious activity is not good either for those who believe in socialism or for those who profess individualism.[191]

Ambedkar aspires for a society based on a common mode of life, in which human dignity and individual integrity may be connected with the principles of social fellowship without any consideration of Caste and creed. That is why he does not wholly rely upon the organization of scientific collectivism, because in it an individual is robbed of his personal freedom, identity and integrity. Equally he avoids the extreme sort of individualism which leads to the exploitation of the masses by few individuals.[192] By rejecting extreme socialism and the extreme individualism, Ambedkar seeks for a new way of life which will synthesize the elements in both socialism and individualism. Thus, the concept of the common good is derived from the supreme values of the individual and social life. For, the common good does not differ in kind from both the individual and

[188] Jatava, *The Social Philosophy of B.R. Ambedkar*, 152.

[189] Keer, *Dr. Ambedkar: Life and Mission*, 26.

[190] Ambedkar, "Annihilation of Caste" 17.

[191] Jatava, *The Social Philosophy of B.R. Ambedkar*, 154.

[192] Ambedkar, "Annihilation of Caste" 47-49.

the social good. It is in substance only the sum total of the good of all individuals in society. The individual good lies only in participation in the good of the collective whole, i.e., in collective responsibility in society.[193]

Ambedkar realizes the need to include common models and common standards in his concept of common good for the harmonious functioning of the society. "In the absence of common models and common standards," he says, "society cannot be a harmonious whole."[194] According to him, with such different models and standard it is impossible for the individual to attain consistency of mind; and a society, which rests upon the supremacy of one group over another, irrespective of its rational or proportionate claims inevitably leads to conflict. He therefore suggests having common rules of morality which are sacred to all, as the only way to avoid such conflicts and disparities.[195]

According to Ambedkar's concept of common good, every individual should have freedom to work for his own welfare, in the atmosphere of harmonious relation between the society and the State. In fact, Ambedkar strove for that kind of community of people, in which each human person shall have the right to bodily protection and shall be guaranteed his rightful place, freedom, and equality.[196] According to him, the foregoing mutuality and congruity between individual and social ends largely depends on respect for law and morality, as he says that "society must have either the sanction of law or the sanction of morality to hold it together. Without either society is sure to go to pieces."[197] He thus conceives law and morality as inseparable companions for establishing a humane, just, rational and moral state.

Ambedkar upholds constitutionalism as the soul of the common good, a humane society. In his moral and social framework he not

---

[193] Jatava, *The Social Philosophy of B.R. Ambedkar*, 155.

[194] B.R. Ambedkar, *The Buddha and His Dhamma* (Bombay: Siddharth College Publication, 1957), 325.

[195] Ambedkar, *The Buddha and his Dhamma*, 325.

[196] Ambedkar, *States and Minorities*, 3.

[197] Jatava, *The Social Philosophy of B.R. Ambedkar*, 156.

only guarantees the individuals liberty of thought and expression but also the all round development of the social patterns, which can link the individual, society and the nation. Constitutionalism, he thinks, will help us in the realization of these ends. In such a state of society, according to him, every industrial and occupational organization can fully function; and there shall be no disparity in legitimate claims between the rightful place of private enterprise and the specific public control.[198]

In this way, Ambedkar protects the individuals, at every level, in every moral and lawful activity, from being uprooted and from falling under the arbitrary power of the State. At the same time, he recognizes that the State must have its own sphere to function in a proper way over the individual interests. The State, according to him, will continue to exist so long as individuals or groups are there. It plays an important role in establishing good relations between one person and another. Thus, according to Ambedkar, the State is only a means for the advancement of human ends in the interest of a better future society.[199] He believes that only a balance between the organizing power of the State and driving force of the free individual can bring about a better society. For, the abolition of individual liberty in the means of production will be unjust, and moreover, a complete socialization or nationalization of the means of production is not practicable as only a balance between them can bring about a better society.[200]

The fundamental basis of Ambedkar's common good is democracy, i.e., the social principles of liberty, equality and fraternity. Jatava quotes him thus:

> … it seems to me that there lies on us a very important duty to see that democracy does not vanish from the earth as a governing principle of human relationship. If we believe in it, we must both be true and loyal to it. We must not only be staunch in our faith in democracy, but we must resolve to see that in whatever we do, we do not help the enemies of

---

[198] Ambedkar, *States and Minorities*, 31-32.

[199] Jatava, *The Social Philosophy of B.R. Ambedkar*, 157.

[200] Jatava, *The Social Philosophy of B.R. Ambedkar*, 157.

> democracy to uproot the principles of liberty, equality and fraternity ... we must strive along with democratic countries to maintain the basis of democratic civilization.[201]

Ambedkar realized that the common good of all individuals, living in society throughout the world, is the need of the hour. His idea of common good is supra-communal, supra-provincial and supra-national. He thus through the common good strove for the realization of social unity of mankind.

3. Democracy - A Way of Life

Unlike other theoreticians, Ambedkar here does not propound any theory of democracy because he looks at democracy not as a fulfillment but as a way of life which is subject to changes and chances of time and events. The concept of democracy as a way of life involves rational empiricism, emphasis on the individual, social endosmosis, the instrumental nature of state, voluntarism, nobility of means, discussion and consents, absence of perpetual rule, and basic equality in all human relations. With deep faith in a democratic outlook on life, Ambedkar lays stress on these requirements of democracy.

Ambedkar regards democracy as a way of life based on an empirical and rational attitude. Rationalism is a strong faith in human reason, its application to social and political relations, whereas empiricism is based on the conviction that all knowledge is derived from human experience. Ambedkar, as a rationalist-empiricist, remarks that there is nothing fixed, nothing eternal: "that everything is changing, that change is the law of life for individuals as well as for society."[202] To him, "everything is vanishing and there is nothing that is permanent in human history."[203] This means that even truth is tentative, changing and subject to constant checking and verification. Truth as a process is changeable in the sense that what it is, is becoming with the constant upbringing new facts to light.

---

[201] Jatava, *The Social Philosophy of B.R. Ambedkar*, 157.

[202] Ambedkar, "Annihilation of Caste" 79.

[203] Ambedkar, *States and Minorities*, 194.

Ambedkar, a true democrat, neither believes in human truth as being absolute nor does he claims, anywhere in his writings, that the statements of facts are true absolutely. He is always inclined to say that under present conditions, his judgment is probably the best one. He prefers an empirical approach in the field of politics, because no person in democracy can claim to be infallible.[204] According to him, no thinking human being can be tied down to a view in the name of consistency; more important than consistency, in a democratic way of life, is social responsibility, for there can be no finality in thinking.[205]

Though democracy has many meanings, yet the supreme test of all political institutions and arrangements is the contribution they make to the all-round growth of every member of society. With this understanding of democracy as a way of life, Ambedkar presupposes social relationships to be founded on the principle of parliamentary system of democracy.[206] In his view, parliamentary democracy produces the best results in the long run, because it assigns great significance to virtues like ability and co-operation, mutual respect and self-help, discipline and devotion to work, for the happiness of the millions of people. It gives chances to all and changes itself as the human needs dictate.[207] To him, only the spirit of the people can help parliamentary democracy to function well as people and democracy are closely related to each other. In his view of democracy, Ambedkar does not want only one section of society or a single party to rule perpetually. To him, "Parliamentary Government means the negation of hereditary rule. No person can claim to be a hereditary ruler. Whoever wants to rule must be elected by the people from time to time."[208] He thus wishes to have a democratic society and government with the consent of public opinion.

Ambedkar holds that a democratic way of life cannot be conceived without an ideal society. He does not limit the concept of

---

[204] Jatava, *The Social Philosophy of B.R. Ambedkar*, 145.

[205] Jatava, *The Social Philosophy of B.R. Ambedkar*, 146.

[206] Jatava, *The Political Philosophy of B.R. Ambedkar*, 93.

[207] Jatava, *The Political Philosophy of B.R. Ambedkar*, 93.

[208] Jatava, *The Social Philosophy of B.R. Ambedkar*, 150.

democracy to a mere form of government but extends it further to a form of social organization. In his own words, "Democracy is not merely a form of government. It is primarily a mode of associated living, of conjoint communicated experience. It is essentially an attitude of respect and reverence towards fellowmen."[209] By this, he means that certain political rights alone do not constitute the basis of democracy. It has to be both social and moral. It must be based on love, friendship and dignity. Sociability and morality are thus the important elements of his concept of democracy.

In his concept of democracy, Ambedkar attaches more importance to society than to the State; but he regards the State as an essential human organization in a democratic way of social life, especially when the society is endangered by disorder and lawlessness. According to him, the State should not interfere so long as the individuals are working well and doing good to one another.[210] Thus the dignity of the individual counts very much in Ambedkar's democratic way of life.

Ambedkar emphasizes on the need of all kinds of freedom so that people may feel and keep themselves in larger liberties. Voluntarism therefore has an important place in his concept of democracy. In democracy, he says, the State should not control every aspect of human life. For him, voluntarism means freedom to form associations and institutions in various fields of life. According to him, people have to be given adequate chances to organize themselves into political parties, educational societies, labour unions, employers associations, economics institutions, etc.[211] Ambedkar thus treats voluntarism as the soul of freedom and democracy. This he hopes will help in strengthening the roots of democracy.

According to him, "The roots of Democracy are to be searched in social relationships, in terms of associated life between the people who form the society."[212] This view of democracy puts an emphasis on the basic equality of human beings. In his social and political

---

[209] Ambedkar, "Annihilation of Caste" 38.

[210] Ambedkar, *States and Minorities*, 9.

[211] Ambedkar, *States and Minorities*, 11-12.

[212] Keer, *Dr. Ambedkar: Life and Mission*, 487.

democracy, all persons have equal rights. All persons have to be considered equal in the eye of the law and every individual is to be given adequate chance to develop and grow. Equality of opportunity and equality of consideration are considered as important factors in his democratic way of life, though complete equality in all respects is not possible.[213]

Ambedkar, while dealing with the concrete problems of human beings and society, thus stands for a democratic form of government. The fundamental elements of his concept of democracy are liberty, equality, fraternity, reason, human experience, the rule of law, natural rights and an emphasis on the individual in social relationships.[214] All these things are necessary from the stand-point of both the general social welfare and the emancipation of human beings as free individuals. The core of his concept of democracy as a way of life is the necessity of the participation of every human being in the formation of social, economic and political values that regulate their lives and keep them together. Thus, by regarding democracy as a way of life, Ambedkar gives it a new dimension which is realized in its humanness, goodness, justice and peace.

4. The Concept of State Socialism

In order to understand Ambedkar's concept of 'State socialism' we need to first look at what socialism means. Jatava explains the concept of socialism as follows:

> Although, socialism is of many types there is one common thread behind all types of socialism. It is that socialism aims at the control of the means of production by the State, i.e., of essential and basic industries, for the equitable distribution of wealth produced. It gives special attention to the interest of the working classes because of their poverty and ignorance. The idea is that social interest should not always be subordinated to individual interest and that the welfare of all be realized without delay.[215]

---

[213] Ambedkar, "Annihilation of Caste" 39-40.

[214] Jatava, *The Social Philosophy of B.R. Ambedkar*, 151.

[215] Jatava, *The Political Philosophy of B.R. Ambedkar*, 127.

For Ambedkar, guild socialism, Christian socialism, scientific socialism, etc., are not very convincing. He accepts the theory of state socialism with necessary modifications in its content and method in the light of Indian cultural tradition.

With a hope to secure a better society, Ambedkar stands for the emancipation of the poorer sections of Indian society, which is hardly possible without some State control. He therefore suggests that 'State socialism' is the need of the hour. The main purpose of State is to put "an obligation on the State to plan the economic life of the people on line, which would lead to the highest point of productivity without closing every avenue to private enterprise, and also provide for the equitable distribution of wealth."[216]

In the economic order, Ambedkar accepts the law of private property with some restraints upon its earnings of increment. According to him, this is possible only through State control over the key industrial undertakings. "State socialism", he says, "is essential for the rapid industrialization of India. Private enterprise cannot do it and if it did, it would produce those inequalities of wealth which private capitalism has produced in Europe and which should be a warning to Indians."[217] His concept of State socialism differs from the State socialists like Rodbertus and Lassale on the questions of capitalist system and private property. He does not want the annihilation of these two institutions, but stands for an effective check upon their irregularities against the interest of the poor working class. He accepts their stress on the need of State intervention, but not to the extent to which they do. He does not want the total destruction of any class, but the actual reformation of the class structure so that the economic benefit may reach the doors of all persons.[218] He thus gives way to individual incentive for the economic well-being of the people.

Though Ambedkar believes in the theory of State socialism, yet he differs from the traditional view at major points. The old view is that share of 'State ownership' should be equal to that of private

---

[216] Ambedkar, *States and Minorities*, 30.

[217] Jatava, *The Political Philosophy of B.R. Ambedkar*, 128.

[218] Jatava, *The Social Philosophy of B.R. Ambedkar*, 111.

enterprise and the State must be a police State. He does not believe either in the equalization of spheres of private and public ownership or in the efficacy of police state.[219]

Ambedkar, in his theory of State socialism, propose the following plan: "State ownership in agriculture with a collectivized method of cultivation and a modified form of State socialism in the field of industry."[220] According to him, without the supply of capital by the State neither agriculture nor industry can be made to yield better results for the rapid progress of a country like India, where the people, by nature, training and temperament, are greedy and who do not wish to invest their hidden money for the larger industries. State ownership in specific industries is necessary. Further he adds, it is the duty of the State to help those who want to realize the goal of socialism for they can lead India in future to realize its dream of a socialist society.[221]

Ambedkar in his theory of State socialism also proposes the nationalization of insurance companies with a double objective. He says:

> Nationalized Insurance gives the individual greater security than the Private Firm does inasmuch as it pledges the resources of the State as a security for the ultimate payment of his insurance money. It also gives the State the resources necessary for financing its economic planning in the absence of which it would have to resort to borrowing from the money market at a high rate of interest.[222]

Ambedkar not only defends human beings' right to private possession and property but also stands for a greater security of the individual's economic interest with the help of State control. In fact, many insurance companies failed in India, and, thus, instead of helping the people, discouraged them. This is why, to him, unless the Government takes some responsibility, people cannot be happy

---

[219] Jatava, *The Social Philosophy of B.R. Ambedkar*, 111.

[220] Ambedkar, *States and Minorities*, 31.

[221] Jatava, *The Political Philosophy of B.R. Ambedkar*, 128.

[222] Ambedkar, *States and Minorities*, 31.

economically, socially and politically. State socialism is a theory, which has full faith in the wisdom of Government.[223]

Ambedkar's 'State Socialism' is not merely an economic theory but it also has social and moral basis. It is built upon a certain ideal of justice and particular conception of the function of society and of the State. It does not suppress individual liberty and also retains the system of private enterprise, while giving the greatest benefit to the poorer section of society.

Jatava sums up Ambedkar's concept of 'State Socialism' in the following three economic processes of human society.

(i) Adaptation of the key industries and agricultural land to meet the demands of the poorer sections of society;
(ii) Maintenance of the productive resources by the State; and
(iii) A just distribution of the common produce among the different people without any distinction of Caste or creed.[224]

5. Non-violence Method of Social Change

Ambedkar, himself being a great jurist and educationist, believed in peaceful methods to bring about prosperity to the downtrodden communities. He was well aware of 'violence' and 'force' as being erroneous and inhuman methods of social change in a society based on liberty, equality and fraternity. He is of the opinion that normally a human being prefers peaceful means to bring about the new social order in the process of social change. He disregards the revolutionary method of social change which disturbs peace and tranquility and creates chaos, strife and war.

Hence, Ambedkar stresses that the organization of the new society should not rest on violence, contempt and hatred. Indeed, it is futile to think in terms of a society, which can be developed for the welfare of all on the foundations of violence, force and compulsion. Such an approach, he emphasizes, is totally unscientific and immoral.[225]

---

[223] Jatava, *The Political Philosophy of B.R. Ambedkar*, 129.

[224] Jatava, *The Social Philosophy of B.R. Ambedkar*, 117.

[225] B.R. Ambedkar, "Buddhism and Communism". Speech at the closing session of the Fourth Conference of the World Fellowship of Buddhist in the State

5.1. Social Change through Peace and Persuasion

Ambedkar, the chief architect of the constitution of modern India, never advocated violence to bring about a social change or a new society based on liberty, equality and fraternity. Even before the present constitutions came into force, he adopted the means of peace and persuasion to achieve the fundamental rights for the poor, the fallen and the weak, which is evident from the following facts.

i) In the pre-independent days he put forward a 'peaceful campaign' to serve civil rights which did not involve any kind of violence against those who denied the fundamental thoughts of life, liberty and happiness.[226]
ii) He said that social reformers should create public opinion in condemnation of existing 'gross inequalities', and they should establish 'bureaus' to deal with urgent cases of inequality. The bureaus might seek to persuade the powerful section of society to give a chance to the poor and the depressed classes, to serve in their shops, factories and mills.[227]
iii) He suggested a common participation on the family level, among the different classes of the people, particularly the Touchable and the Untouchable Hindus. This involves the establishment of a closer contact between the two. "The live contact thus established", he says, "will familiarize both to a common and associated life and will pave the way for the unity, which we are all striving after."[228]
iv) He emphasized the employment of a huge army of workers to carry out the programme against Caste and Untouchability. But he was against mercenary workers who could not show sincerity of purpose in discharging their duties. Instead he

---

Gallery Hall in Kathmandu (Nepal) on 20th November 1956. As cited in D.R. Jatava, *The Social Philosophy of B.R. Ambedkar* (Agra: Phoenix Publication House, 1965), 118.

[226] B.R. Ambedkar, *Pakistan or the Partition of India* (Bombay: Thacker and Co. Ltd, 1946), 135-136.

[227] Ambedkar, *Pakistan or the Partition of India*, 136.

[228] Ambedkar, *Pakistan or the Partition of India*, 138.

> favored the employment of the workers who regarded social service as 'love's labour.'[229]

Ambedkar thus wanted a social change not through force and violence but essentially by love, peace and persuasion.

5.2. Social Change through Legislation

It is our common experience that social change through a change of heart often takes a very long time to actualize itself. Even an intellectual recognition of the urgent need for such a change and the appreciation of its sublimity fails to reconcile many die-hards to the actual process of change. In such cases, the reformers have necessarily to resort to legislation, for legislation, too, falls within the ambit of peaceful, constitutional change.[230] The example of such a legislative change proposed by Ambedkar is the introduction of the 'Hindu Code Bill' through an act of legislation in 1950. The main aim of this Bill was to reform and to bring about radical and fundamental changes in Hindu society through legislative means.[231]

Ambedkar is thus striving for a new social order by peace, love and goodwill, through actual living or, wherever necessary, through an act of legislature. His advocacy of non-violence along with the democratic way of life is highly commendable in the existing conditions of strife and war. Without this method, social harmony and intellectual freedom cannot be preserved. Thus, non-violence also emerges as one of the main features of his philosophy of Social Humanism.

---

[229] Ambedkar, *Pakistan or the Partition of India*, 139.

[230] Jatava, *The Social Philosophy of B.R. Ambedkar*, 97.

[231] Keer, *Dr. Ambedkar: Life and Mission*, 414-415.

Chapter 6

The Critics of Ambedkar

Ambedkar has played an important role in the freedom movement and emancipation of the Untouchables in the country. The dominant theme of this movement was to inculcate a spirit of self-help and dignity in the downtrodden in order to secure social and political rights in the future sot up of this nation. Although, many groups of leaders and organizations wanted him to be their camp-follower, he preferred to be an independent person. He always felt that the orthodox reactionary group wanted to exercise their control and supervision over the struggle of the downtrodden in order to fulfill their vested interests. He did not favor to base the Untouchable's upliftment movement merely on the grounds of charity and compassion, as other social reformers of 19th and 20th centuries did. According to him, social equality was not a question of begging from the high-ups. Instead he asserted that the Untouchables were entitled to it as a matter of right, as citizens of the country.

Ambedkar was a man of action who wanted to find solutions to problems that faced his community and India as well. Always a controversial figure, his statements, speeches and voluminous writings on diverse subjects invariably provoked not only a great deal of thinking, but also a lot of conflict and controversy. His outburst against Hindu orthodoxy aroused deep anger among the Caste Hindu leaders paving the way for bitter protests. His realistic way of analyzing things and issues created storms. In the present chapter I will try to analyze the various issues, viewpoints, conflicts and criticism of Gandhi and the Marxists, with regard to Ambedkar's thought which will facilitate a better understanding of his philosophy.

1. Gandhi and the other Staunch Hindus

Since the days of his early life, Ambedkar was a critic of Hindu social order especially with regard to Caste and Untouchability. He revolted against the continuance of Caste division and the practice of Untouchability, because these reduced millions of people to a sub-human status. He therefore launched and movement for the abolition of Caste and Untouchability.

According to him, the root of Caste-Untouchability ridden society was the social ideal based on Chaturvarnya, i.e., the four-fold classification of all men into the Brahmins, the Kshatriyas, the Vaishyas and the Shudras. He says: "There cannot be a more degrading system of social organization than Chaturvarnya. It is the system which deadens, paralyses and cripples the people from helpful activity."[232] He therefore strove for the total annihilation of Varna Vyavastha. He suggested practice of inter-Caste dining and inter-Caste marriage as a step towards the abolition of Caste system. These measures were clearly inadequate since these customs were governed by belief in the Shastras. He therefore remarks: "The real remedy is to destroy the belief in the sanctity of the Shastras. How do you expect to succeed, if you allow the Shastras to continue to mould the beliefs and opinions of the people?"[233] The conservative Hindus who upheld 'Varna-dharma and the divine Shastras' as the basis of Hinduism, could not tolerate Ambedkar's criticism against it. They therefore created a strong opposition against Ambedkar and his social reform movement.

---

[232] Ambedkar, *Annihilation of Caste*, 65.

[233] Ambedkar, *Annihilation of Caste*, 74.

Almost all social and religious reformers through the ages criticized Caste and Untouchability. However, no conservative Hindu cared about the criticism voiced by these persons. It is because, unlike Ambedkar, they did not dare to criticize the very roots of Hinduism, i.e., the Varna system. Instead they remained with the criticism of the apparent effect of the system. Many of them, such as Bhagawan Das, Swami Dayanand, even went to the extent of upholding Varna Vyavastha as a remedy to social evil prevalent in India.[234] As they wanted to abolish Caste and Untouchability without altering the Varna system and since most of them upheld the authority of Shastras and Varna system, they were hailed as the saviors of Hindu culture and religion. On the contrary, Ambedkar was condemned as a fanatic and iconoclast. Had he criticized only Caste and Untouchability like others, no conservative Hindu would have opposed him; but since he struck at the root in order to destroy the sick tree in its entirety, he invited the wrath of all conservative and orthodox Hindus.[235]

Mahatma Gandhi was among the first few to raise the voice in defense of what Ambedkar protested against. Gandhi once remarked: "Dr. Ambedkar is a challenge to Hinduism."[236] He was of the view that there was no link between the Varna system and Caste and Untouchability. Gandhi argued:

> The Vedas, Upanishads, Smritis and Puranas including Ramayana and Mahabharata are the Hindu Scriptures… who is the best interpreter? Not learned men surely. Learning there must be. But religion does not live by it. It lives in the experiences of its saints and seers, in their lives and sayings. Varna and Ashrama are institutions which have nothing to do with Castes. The law of Varna teaches us that each one of us has to earn our bread by following the ancestral calling. It defines not our rights, but our duties… And there is nothing

---

[234] R.A. Prasad, *Socialist Thought in Modern India* (Meerut: Meenakshi Publications, 1974), 13 and 27.

[235] D.R. Jatava, *The Critics of Dr. Ambedkar* (New Delhi: Bhartiya Shoshit Jan Uttan Parishad, 1975), 5.

[236] Jatava, *The Critics of Dr. Ambedkar*, 5.

> in the law of Varna to warrant a belief in Untouchability. A religion has to be judged not by its worst specimens but by the best it might have produced.[237]

Gandhi argued further: "If Caste and Varna are convertible terms and if Varna is an integral part of the Shastras which define Hinduism, I do not know how a person who rejects Caste, i.e., Varna, can call himself a Hindu."[238]

Ambedkar objected to what Gandhi argued for, by saying that the masses did not know the contents of the Shastras. They believed in what they were told by the saints and seers. But he said: "The saints have never, according to my study, carried on a campaign against Caste and Untouchability. They were not concerned with the relation between man and God. They did not preach that all men were equal. They preached that all men were equal in the eyes of God – a very different and a very innocuous proposition which nobody can find difficult to preach or dangerous to believe in."[239] Ambedkar thus holds on to his view that Varna and Caste are evil ideas and it is not possible to remove Caste and Untouchability without demolishing the authority of Varna-dharma as enshrined in the Shastras.

Gandhi's insistence on the Varna-dharma was unacceptable to Ambedkar, who, by his experience, knew its inherent weaknesses. To him, Varna-dharma was the root of Caste and Untouchability; but for Gandhi it had nothing to do with them. "Broadly speaking, the difference between Gandhi's and Ambedkar's approach was the result of one viewing the problem from above and the other from below. While Gandhi wanted the structure to remain the same with its four divisions, Ambedkar wanted the entire structure to change on the basis of equality. Thus, Gandhi devoted his energies to changing the heart of the Hindus and made it clear that there was no place in

---

[237] M. K. Gandhi, "Dr. Ambedkar's Indictment", *Harijan*, July 18, 1936. As cited in D.R. Jatava, *The Critics of Dr. Ambedkar* (New Delhi: Bhartiya Shoshit Jan Uttan Parishad, 1975), 6.

[238] Gandhi, "Dr. Ambedkar's Indictment", 6.

[239] Ambedkar, *Annihilation of Caste*, 112-113.

his programme for the educated, politically conscious Untouchable fighting for his civil rights."[240]

Ambedkar's vigorous campaign against Varnaism and Brahmanism made the orthodox Hindus his critics in his life time, but he was never deterred by the criticism of his opponents. He did not confine his attacks on Hindu religious system to verbal outbursts but went ahead to become a man of dynamic action. His act of burning of Manusmruti – a symbol of inequality, cruelty and injustice, on December 25, 1927, in Mahad satyagraha, aroused deep anger and bitter protests by the orthodox and conservative Hindus.[241] Ambedkar's attack on Hindu Scriptures, his Satyagrahas and above all, the bonfire of Manusmriti provoked ill-feelings in the minds of the orthodox and staunch Hindus who were alarmed at these actions and Ambedkar became a most hated person in India. He was called a fanatic, denounced as an enemy of Hindus and termed as a destroyer of Hinduism. They criticized him because he drove the Untouchables to adopt a militant policy.[242]

Ambedkar continued to do his work by calling the suppressed humanity to rise in revolt against the age-old slavery and to have equal status in Indian society with others. The conservatives and orthodox Hindus were faced with a man who not only shook the foundation of the Varna-system and Brahmanism but also inculcated a spirit of freedom in the dehumanized millions to effect change in their ancestral faith.[243] His renunciation of the belief in Hindu gods, pilgrimages, fasts and scriptures provoked anger in orthodox and staunch Hindus as it meant loosening of their grip and domination over Untouchables whom they had been exploiting for their political and social ends.[244] He went to the extent of moving the famous Hindu code bill in Indian Parliament so as to free women from their

[240] Yashodhara Dalmia, "Scheduled Castes – A View from below", *The Times of India*, December 15, 1974. As cited in D.R. Jatava, *The Critics of Dr. Ambedkar* (New Delhi: Bhartiya Shoshit Jan Uttan Parishad, 1975), 6.

[241] Ambedkar, *Annihilation of Caste*, 70.

[242] Jatava, *The Critics of Dr. Ambedkar*, 21.

[243] Keer, *Dr. Ambedkar: Life and Mission*, 233-234.

[244] Jatava, *The Critics of Dr. Ambedkar*, 22.

age-old slavery. This created confusion in the house and the house was divided on this issue. The orthodox section in Parliament and outside criticized Ambedkar for his radical move to reform Hindu society.[245] On his call for change and urbanization many of the Untouchables started changing their old habits and dirty professions. Some of them even shifted to the cities and settled there to live respectable lives. This meant meaningful reorganization and the change in the structure of the society on the part of the conservative Hindus, which added to their frustration.[246]

Thus the staunch and reactionary Hindus tried to block every action of Ambedkar. They criticized him for every step that he took for the social reform of the Hindu society. They were opposed to the reform of Hindu society along with its Shastras and Varna system which led them to criticize Ambedkar and his movement for the freedom and upliftment of the Untouchables.

2. The Orthodox Marxists

Like the Orthodox and staunch Hindus, the orthodox Marxists too opposed and criticized Ambedkar, for their own reasons. Perhaps, they did not like his philosophy of life, particularly his influence on the downtrodden section of Indian masses in the sphere of religion and politics. Although, Ambedkar appreciated Marx's ideas and Lenin's zeal for the uplift of toiling classes, still it was not possible for him to subscribe fully to the Communist ideology, due to following points of differences in their ideologies.

2.1. Religion as the Opium of People

Marxism considers religion to be 'the opium of the people', and for the Marxists, religion is distress in the sheer form of spiritual aroma. The abolition of religion, or the illusory happiness of the people as they say, is essentially required for their real happiness.[247] However, Ambedkar did not agree with this anti-religious and irreligious outlook on life. He held that religion was a part of one's social life

[245] Jatava, *The Critics of Dr. Ambedkar*, 23.

[246] Jatava, *The Critics of Dr. Ambedkar*, 23.

[247] Marx and Engels. *On Religion* (Moscow: Progress Publishers, 1957), 41-42.

or inheritance; one's life and dignity and pride were bound up with it. He believed in the social force of religion; and that force lay in religion being a unified system of beliefs and practices.[248]

The Marxist condemnation of religion, in fact, had some grain of truth in it. For in the name of religion, all sorts of atrocities and hypocrisies were committed against innocent people in the past and still, inhuman treatment is given to some sections of society in the name of sanctity of Shastras. It was made an instrument of oppression and exploitation. What the Marxists condemned as religion was also condemned by Ambedkar. What they meant by the opium of the people was not to be found in his concept of religion. Ambedkar's concept of religion had a close link with social morality, people's empirical welfare. It was essentially a system of right relations and was entirely based on social ethics, i.e., liberty, equality and fraternity. It is for a human being's own good that he must follow these principle.[249] Ambedkar's concept of religion was essentially a humanist approach toward human relations.

2.2. Clash in the field of Morality

There is also a major clash in the field of morality between Marxism and Ambedkar. The Marxist morality is based on class-structure of a society. Lenin said: "Our morality is entirely subordinated to interests of the class struggle of the proletariat. Our morality is derived from the interests of the class struggle of the proletariat."[250]

The Marxist concept of morality, which safeguards the interest of the proletariat, was not acceptable to Ambedkar as it was not truly a human morality. He observed that the Marxist made the same mistake which the capitalists did by adhering to their own morality. Class-morality was always liable to lead to conflict, because it would mean that every class would prescribe its own morality, the sectarian principles, and would justify its actions even if they were wrong and

---

[248] B.R. Ambedkar, "Buddha and the future of his religion", 1950 as cited in D.R. Jatava, *The Critics of Dr. Ambedkar* (New Delhi: Bhartiya Shoshit Jan Uttan Parishad, 1975), 13.

[249] Jatava, *The Political Philosophy of B.R. Ambedkar*, 182-186.

[250] Jatava, *The Critics of Dr. Ambedkar*, 27.

harmful for their members of the society.[251] He remarks that, instead the morality based on the common principles, would create social cohesion.[252] According to him, the common, universal and sacred rules of morality would protect not only the best, but also the weak, and would safeguard the growth of the individual.[253]

2.3. Economic Determinism

Another thesis of Marxism is that history is determined by economic forces, i.e., economic determinism is the truth of all social evolution. Ambedkar did not deny that economic forces had an important role to play, yet he was not prepared to accept that they were the only factors to determine the course of history. He remarked that in essence it was a human being who was responsible for a just and unjust social order and the economic forces. He also did not accept the Marxists' and the Socialists' view that economic changes could alter India's social system. According to him its roots lay in religion and not in property relations.[254]

2.4. Dictatorship of the Proletariat

The Marxist political theory is based on the dictatorship of the proletariat, one party system, and totalitarian structure of state and government. The whole Marxist political theory was unacceptable to Ambedkar, because he had profound respect for parliamentary democracy, though it suffered from its own weaknesses, in the social milieu in which it had to function.[255]

Thus, Ambedkar, a true liberal democrat, never wished to be a Marxist, because he rejected the basic ideas of Marxist philosophy such as economic determinism, anti-religionism, dictatorship of the proletariat, dialectical materialism and one party system.

Since Marxist ideology was in no way acceptable to Ambedkar as an alternative to Varnaism and Brahmanism, he embraced Buddhism.

---

[251] Jatava, *The Political Philosophy of B.R. Ambedkar*, 194.

[252] Ambedkar, *The Buddha and His Dhamma*, 325.

[253] Ambedkar, *The Buddha and His Dhamma*, 325-335.

[254] Jatava, *The Critics of Dr. Ambedkar*, 29-30.

[255] Jatava, *The Critics of Dr. Ambedkar*, 30-31.

He emphatically claimed that 'Buddhism was a complete answer to Marx and his Communism'[256] by saying: "I prefer Buddhism, because it gives three principles in combination which no other religion does. Buddhism teaches prajna (understanding as against superstition and supernaturalism), karuna (love), and samata (equality). This is what man wants for a good and happy life. Neither god nor soul can save the society. Once it is realized that Buddhism is a social gospel, its revival would be an everlasting event."[257]

Ambedkar's conversion to Buddhism and his claim that it was an alternative to Marxism in India greatly disturbed the Marxists. Had he embraced Buddhism in a traditional manner without expressing his views on Marxism and Communism, no Marxist in India would have bothered about it. But since he had asserted that Buddhism was a complete answer to Marxism, this caused annoyance in the intellectual circle of the Indian Marxists who started criticizing Ambedkar.[258]

In Marxists' criticism of Ambedkar three specific points stand out clearly. They are:

i) That Dr. Ambedkar did not cooperate with the nationalist movement in the struggle for liberation and forging a unity between Touchables and Untouchables.
ii) That Ambedkar's movement has weakened the left forces in the country.
iii) That his conversion, instead of solving the problems of the Untouchables, was a leap into escapism.[259]

These charges leveled against Ambedkar have been ruled out by Jatava in the following manner.

i) The history of the National liberation movement was a complex process in which different individuals, leaders and scholars had different roles to play. It was not possible to bring

[256] Jatava, *The Critics of Dr. Ambedkar*, 32.

[257] Keer, *Dr. Ambedkar: Life and Mission*, 499.

[258] Jatava, *The Critics of Dr. Ambedkar*, 33.

[259] Jatava, *The Critics of Dr. Ambedkar*, 33.

together all of them. In fact Congress leaders like Gandhi, Nehru, Tilak, were aiming at only political independence of India while Ambedkar had a different outlook altogether. Although he was not opposed to political reform, he advocated abolition of Caste system and reconstruction of Hindu society on the basis of equality before any political reform. Thus, the basic difference in their ideologies kept them away from joining hands.[260]

ii) The second charge that Ambedkar's movement weakened the left forces in the country could generally be leveled against anyone who does not accept the ideas of leftist ideology. The leftist leadership wanted to make the Untouchables the pawns in the game of power-politics during the pre-independence year as much as today as they have been trying for the social freedom without campaigning against the Caste structure of Hindu society. It is because the Marxist leaders, mostly consisting of upper Caste Hindus, did not dare to wage any war against the evil as of Caste and Untouchability. It is but natural that Ambedkar, the savior of the Untouchables, remained away from the Marxists' movements.[261]

iii) The charge of 'escapism from the real issues by turning to Buddhism' has also been leveled against Ambedkar. As Jatava observes, Ambedkar achieved many great things for his people which the others could not possibly do. Why should he become frustrated when his people became a force to be reckoned with in the mainstream of national life? Jatava further remarks that the charge of escapism could be leveled against a person who is either completely retired from active social life or in a quiet forest undisturbed by the miseries of the world. By embracing Buddhism, Ambedkar sought to create a new way of life for his people. In fact it led him to work more for the people living in the rural areas.[262]

---

[260] Jatava, *The Critics of Dr. Ambedkar*, 36-37.

[261] Jatava, *The Critics of Dr. Ambedkar*, 44-45.

[262] Jatava, *The Critics of Dr. Ambedkar*, 48-50.

Chapter 7

An Evaluation of Ambedkar's Social Philosophy

This book has been an exposition of Ambedkar's humanistic vision of reality. An evaluation of any author or philosopher requires that the critics review what he has actually said. Genuine or creative criticism exists in order to fan the fires of original genius. It is then appropriate as well as imperative, that I conclude this study with a review of Ambedkar's overall socio-politico-philosophical vision of humanity. These concluding remarks are meant to serve this purpose. We shall first look at the positive elements of his contribution and then also point out some of the grey areas which can or need to be worked upon in his philosophy.

1. Positive Elements of Ambedkar's Contribution

1.1. The Context of Ambedkar's Philosophy

Every thinker philosophizes within a context and background. Before Ambedkar, many liberal Hindu reformers like Ranade, Tilak, Gandhi, etc., preached the ideology of social equality. Since all these reformers belonged to the upper Caste society and lived its culture, they failed to see the problems of the Untouchables at the grass root level. The context of Ambedkar is unique in this regard. The other reformers looked at the 'Caste-Untouchability' situation from outside. Ambedkar, being an Untouchable himself, had the advantage of understanding and becoming part of the problems of the lower Caste people. He had lived and outgrown these social conditions to reach the academic heights and to become the chief architect of India's Constitutions. It is from within this socio-cultural context that Ambedkar lives and philosophizes.

1.2. Ambedkar – A Social Humanist

As a humanist, Ambedkar's chief concern in life was to meet the challenges of wrongly idealized social relations which threatened the whole of human existence and shook the foundations of a moral and just social order. He saw clearly that the prevailing ethical and political drawbacks sprang from a total misconception of the meaning of human relationship, and the problem of right human relations was the key to his entire thoughts and actions. The aim of his mission was to arouse in men and women the passion for right relations. His purpose was practical rather than speculative and his philosophy of life was essentially a development and evolution under the conditions and events that prevailed in Indian society. As a spokesman of ignored humanity, he created human rights for all and tried to bring all human beings on a par socially. His aim was not communal and limited to personal benefits but it was essentially social and human, related to all who suffered from slavery, injustice, tyranny and exploitation. He broke the shackles of traditionalism, religious orthodoxy and blind superstition; he stood for human dignity and freedom, for simplicity, integrity, liberty, equality, social and economic justice, material prosperity and spiritual discipline. In his thoughts and actions he always attempted a harmony between an individual and society, the two poles of his philosophical attitude. Thus Ambedkar's thoughts - social, political and moral – leave no doubt that he is a true social humanist.

1.3. Concern for the Upliftment of the Untouchables

Ambedkar is criticized for being a self-centered person, when he proposed the social freedom of the Untouchables at the cost of political freedom of India from the British rule. He is also criticized because of his excessive favoritism to the Untouchables. In fact at time it appeared as if there were no other people besides the 'Untouchables' for Ambedkar. His battle for the cause of the Untouchables is justified since he had lived and experienced the caste tyranny, suppression and humiliation of Caste Hindus towards the Untouchables. His theories about the origin of Untouchability and the Shudras were and are controversial, but his efforts to solve the problem are note worthy. He expressed the sorrows of the Untouchables, tried to channel the activities of the depressed classes and bring out a force which would challenge the whole Caste-ridden and Untouchable bound society. In mobilizing them, he created a sense of self-respect and pride in them, asked them to uproot this society which perpetuated social justice. All his actions were geared towards the elevation of Untouchables in social, political and economic fields. Thus, for him, success in life meant success in raising the depressed classes to the status of human beings.

1.4. A Wholistic Concept of Ideal Society

Ambedkar's concept of ideal society is most suited to the needs of modern Indian society. For him, society is an integrated whole and each individual is tied with another in an indissoluble relationship. His view of society fully agrees that an individual is mainly responsible for his own welfare, at the same time, he shares the collective responsibility for the good of the society. This sense of collective responsibility is the main feature of his integrated view of social life, which involves the essential elements of his philosophy of Social Humanism – liberty, equality and fraternity.

1.5. Preference of Social Freedom over Political Freedom

Like any other social reformer of his time, Ambedkar too strived for the realization of national freedom. What he was more interested in was the internal freedom or social freedom for the Untouchables from the slavery of the Caste Hindus. He had understood that even after the political freedom of India, the condition of the Untouchables would remain very much the same. He therefore strived towards the social freedom of his people from the clutches of Caste and Untouchability more than the political freedom of the country.

1.6. Ambedkar – A Great Educationist

Ambedkar fully believed that education was the only saviour of the down-trodden people without which there would be no salvation for this unfortunate section of people of India. He therefore advised and firmly told them to use education as a weapon to cut down their social slavery and to gain social status, economic betterment and political freedom. His efforts to educate these people, by opening up various educational institutions and offering educational facilities, prove himself to be the greatest educationist of his time.

1.7. Ambedkar – A Modern Manu

Ambedkar was a many-sided genius. As he went ahead in life, his innumerable talents came forth to prove his genius. He was thus a distinguished economist, a learned professor, a brilliant lawyer, a reputed author and a great political leader, but above all he was a prophet of self-help and self-respect for millions of low Caste people. Following these principles he himself rose to international eminence and exhorted his community to follow these principles as the only effective way of removing their disabilities. His contribution to the Constitutions of India is undoubtedly of the highest order. Indeed, he was a modern Manu and deserves to be called the father or the chief architect of the Constitutions of India. His was a life of dedication, sincerity and service, and in his career he proved that a persons worth did not depend on riches, high birth and good connections.

1.8. Concern for Humanity – The Singular Thrust of Ambedkar's thought

There will be no exaggeration in saying that Ambedkar's biography is the history of the struggle for the emancipation of the millions of Untouchables in India from perpetual degradation and misery. His life is the saga of a heroic fight for establishing basic human values in society. He was a humanist who was intensely human even beyond humanity. Although, he was a great politician and has made an intellectual contribution to India's political revolution, still the roots of his humanism can be traced to his total identification with the problem of Untouchability. One should not be surprised if he is recognized as one of the great emancipators of humanity in history.

1.9. Ambedkar's Original and Creative Contribution

The most significant and applicable contribution of Ambedkar is his humanistic conception of the social reality. The originality of Ambedkar consists in his ability to explore into existing social and human traditions and to discover their insights which could serve to express his own humanistic vision of reality. His understanding of ideal society, democracy-as a way of life, non-violent method of social change and his concepts of common good and state socialism are his gift of synthesis and creative reflection. It gives us the new vision towards the relationship between one person and another, individual and society, and the society as a whole. Besides this, his efforts to present the critique of Hindu social order and his reflection on religious conversion too are remarkably creative.

So far I have hightlighted the 'positive' elements of Ambedkar's contribution, i.e., his insights on social humanism, to the philosophical world at large. The evaluation of his social philosophy along with its strengths also calls us to be aware of certain 'weak points' or the 'grey areas' which can or need to be improved upon in his philosophy.

2. Grey Areas in the Philosophy of Ambedkar

2.1. Misunderstanding of Hinduism

We have already seen the various aspects of Ambedkar's vision of an ideal society. The social behavior pattern created by Caste and Untouchability seem to have prejudiced him even against some merits of Hinduism. His concept of society fails to distinguish between what Hinduism 'is' and what Hinduism 'has been', in the sense of Caste-behaviour pattern. His criticism of what Hinduism has been should be welcomed and admitted willingly because from a humanistic point of view, a large section of Hindu society (consisting of the Shudras and the Untouchables) was deprived of its legitimate and human rights to education, property and arms. In ancient Vedic culture, at its best, Hinduism was another name for the principles of hospitality in assimilating different cultures of the world.[263] Hence his condemnation of the whole of Hinduism, viz., what it essentially and ideally is or what the Vedic Dharma is at its best in principle, cannot be sustained. What Hinduism is, is quite different from what Hinduism has been. Therefore by rejecting what is for what has been Ambedkar seems to have misunderstood the meaning of both.

In his anger against the Hindus and eagerness to secure a separate communal status for the Scheduled Caste, Ambedkar overlooked many far-reaching problems of social and economic reconstruction. The most important of them is the future of the Caste. In order to uplift the poor and down trodden of the society, he wanted to do away with the Caste system. However, he failed to realize that Caste was an inseparable part of Hinduism and therefore by the destruction of the Caste system of Hindu society he was actually trying for the destruction of 'Hinduism' as a religion, which was a practical impossibility.

2.2. Inapplicability of Ambedkar's Concept of 'State Socialism'

Through his concept of 'state socialism' Ambedkar endeavoured to strike a balance between the central authority of the State and the liberty of the individual. According to him, a State was practical and realistic when it provided the practical needs of the people. He could not fully realize his concept of state socialism because of the age-old but wrong tradition that land belongs to the people, and not to the State. People are afraid that State control may endanger the full play of mass labour. Therefore, Ambedkar's ideal of nationalization of agriculture is conceived as hardly practicable or realizable.

2.3. Conversion Movement – A Failure

Knowing the pros and cons of conversion, having made constitutional safeguards to Hindu Untouchables, Ambedkar took a decision for

[263] Jatava, *The Social Philosophy of B.R. Ambedkar*, 100.

religious conversion. By this act of his he staked the future of lakhs of Untouchable converts to Buddhism. Today after the death of Ambedkar, one observes that the world Buddhist society has not really assimilated India's Neo-Buddhists. The Neo-Buddhists today do not receive the same treatment from their Buddhist brethren, which was expected of them by Ambedkar in his time. The conversion movement to Buddhism has neither succeeded in removing the 'Untouchability' stigma of the Untouchables nor has it offered the equal social status to the Untouchable converts to Buddhism as the other Buddhists. The question that arises now is that – if conversion cannot resolve Caste differences why Ambedkar should have led a conversion movement even as he provided constitutional safeguards to strengthen the economic and educational background of Scheduled Caste? Because of all these reasons his process of conversion proved its inadequacy and ineffectiveness as a weapon to ameliorate the conditions of the downtrodden Untouchables and maintain social equality. That is why the idea of conversion was not taken up by the Untouchables as a class. On the contrary, some of his followers opposed his programme of conversion on ideological and practical grounds.

2.4. The Negative Effects of Ambedkar's Favoritism towards the Upliftment of the Untouchables

Ambedkar was fighting for a separate electorate for the Untouchables which meant separation of the Untouchables from the Hindu community. It was just what the British wanted to foster their policy of 'divide and rule'. In a way, it appeared that Ambedkar was collaborating with them.

In order to safeguard the interest of the lower classes of Indian society Ambedkar wanted foreign rule to continue in India. For this purpose he even went to the extent of opposing the Indian National Congress and particularly its demand for independence. Through this act of his, Ambedkar's biased attitude for the sake of Untouchable community, at the cost of Indian freedom, emerges very clearly. From this his humanistic vision of reality appears to be limited to the Untouchables and the other low Caste communities.

2.5. Lack of Perception in the Formation of the Coherent Dalit Community

The Dalits today do not form an all-India community with a common language, religion or any other special characteristic. They inter-dine and inter-marry only within their own local Castes and sub-Caste. They are distributed evenly in all districts, talukas and villages and form a minority everywhere. Under any system of provincial autonomy, their main interests will be bound up with the provincial governments. Ambedkar would like to make them a coherent all-India community like the Muslims, Anglo-Indians or Indian Christians. It appears to be a social and political impossibility.

Chapter 8

Conclusion

The social philosophy of Ambedkar appears to be more challenging now than ever before. We will see how it is challenging us in the present world-situation. I shall also explain briefly how I, as a Christian, see his challenge to the Church in India.

In our country today, if we look around, we find that there is widespread violation of every kind of human rights. The fundamental rights to food, shelter, health care and social security are denied to the majority of the people. On the other hand, civil rights are granted more in theory. In practice, it is the rich and the powerful that are able to avail themselves of them. Equality before the law in principle goes together with gross inequality in practice. There are several traditional handicaps for women and Dalit section of the population. Some of these even seem to be aggravated as time goes on. The basic rights of the vast number of working children are grossly neglected. Democratic rights are violated by such means as money, power and wholesale misinformation.

The age-old problems of Casteism and Untouchability are still in existence today. When the Constitution of India outlawed

Untouchability in 1955, many national leaders believed that a centuries old practice had been brought to an end.[264] But now, nearly sixty three years later, there is no total success of the statutory measure. Millions of Dalits across the country who account for roughly 1/5th of the population continue to suffer birth-based discrimination and humiliation. In fact, Untouchability has not only survived the constitutional ban but has taken new avatars in many parts of the state.[265] Although on the superficial level we speak of the values like justice, equality and liberty, on the deeper level we see the great amount of indifference with regard to it prevalent in our existing situation. It is seventy years since we have received political independence but how many of us really enjoy the social independence within our country or can live freely in the society, is still a question today. Even though necessary provisions have been made in our Constitutions to enhance the upliftment of the poor, downtrodden and backward class people, yet we have not succeeded in implementing them in our daily life. If any liberal person does

---

[264] Article 17 of Indian Constitution abolishes and forbids untouchability in any form. At the same time, it also makes it an offence punishable as per the law made by the Parliament. In order to fulfill the mandate of Article 17 of the Constitution, the Parliament enacted the Untouchability (Offences) Act, 1955. "Untouchability in India" http://www.azadindia.org/social-issues/untouchability-in-india.html Accessed on 25/4/2018.

[265] According to National Campaign on Dalit Human Rights (NCDHR), there are various forms of discriminations being practiced against Dalits in India. Some of these are:

- Prohibited from eating with other Caste members,
- Prohibited from marrying with other Caste members,
- Discriminatory seating arrangements and separate utensils in restaurants,
- Segregation in seating and food arrangements in village functions and festivals,
- Prohibited from wearing sandals or holding umbrellas in front of dominant Caste members,
- Prohibited from using common village path,
- Separate burial grounds,
- No access to village's common/public properties and resources (wells, ponds, temples, etc.)
- "Untouchability in India" http://www.indiacelebrating.com/social-issues/untouchability-in-india/ Acessed on 25/4/2018.

come forward to bring them to our notice, the 'orthodox' of the society do not hesitate to foil their attempts and to crush them down.

The social philosophy of Ambedkar, based on the principles of liberty, equality and fraternity, shows us the way in such a situation. His 'social philosophy' challenges us to break away the shackles of bondage, inequality, and injustice and to become free 'human beings'. It shows us the path of 'social humanism' which leads to the creation of justice, peace and harmony in society. His insights on the creation of a new social order demand from us the reformation of the age-old, Caste-ridden social order which is in fact the need of the hour.

As a Christian, I personally see his philosophy as a challenge posed to the Church in India today. Through the explorations of the lives of the Christian Dalit converts Ambedkar has brought to light the attitude of indifference that the Church in India, especially the 'high Caste Christians' are having towards them. While exposing the hypocrisy of the Church in India he shows us how on the one hand it preaches Jesus' message of 'equality', 'love' and 'brotherhood' and on the other hand some of its members overcome by the spirit of 'Casteism' degrade and despise the Dalit Christians. His critical examination of the social conditions of the Dalit Christians is an eye-opener to all the Indian Christians. He is thus challenging them to be true to their faith and to the social teaching of their founder Jesus Christ.

In Latin America we have seen the Christian priests coming up with the idea of social justice which later on came forth as theology of liberation and was developed in the context of the exploitation of the poor. Today, in India too, we need to create this sort of movement of liberation – liberation from age-old religious traditions, evil practices of Casteism, social inequality, injustice and subhuman treatment given to the downtrodden of the society.

While Dalit theology has taken root in Indian context, it needs to be directed properly so that it will be the meeting point of Christian faith and Indian reality in its totality. Such an undertaking will demand twofold loyalty: loyalty to Christian faith and revelation, and loyalty to the reality in which we live; i.e., the traditions, contemporary problems and the aspirations of people around us. While the eruption of the Dalit movement is gaining momentum within the Indian Church, the Dalit Christians have begun to demand their legitimate rights. At this historical moment the Church should welcome Dalit theology as a transforming grace for the Indian Church.[266]

Today there is indeed an increased awareness and consciousness of social responsibility in the Catholic Church in India. According to Archbishop Emeritus Alphonse Mathias, who was the President of the Catholic Bishops Conference of India from 1989 to 1994, the deepest concerns of the bishops in India today are the upliftment of the Dalits, providing a voice to the unorganized labour and granting women their due status.[267]

After the Second Vatican Council, numerous seminars and consultations which have taken place in India have brought about the wave of new awareness of social responsibility in the Church. There has been a great amount of dedication and involvement on the part of the Catholic Church in helping the poor through the various developmental and social projects. Besides organized developmental works, there has been a deepening of thought and a widening of perspectives as regard the liberative role the Church should play in the concrete situations of poverty and misery of the people in our country.[268]

Still the Church has not given clear orientation towards issues like Caste system, exploitation of women, bonded labour and the exploitation of tribals in India. The Church has maintained her silence on the issues of land reform and movement on the distribution of land. The Church in India, in spite of her statements and her commitment to be a Church to serve, a Church for the poor and of the poor, is highly institutional in her structure and character. This heavy institutionalization of the Church does not fully permit its personnel to be fully involved in struggles for social justice and social

---

[266] "Dalit Theology: A Transforming Grace for the Indian Church" https://www.scribd.com/document/300019581/Dalit-Theology Accessed on 25/4/2018.

[267] Editorial, "The Bishops' Concerns" *The Examiner*, vol. 143, January 25, 1992, 1.

[268] Baptist Menezes, "Response of the Indian Church to Social Issues" *Indian Theological Studies*, Sept-Dec' 91, 275-279.

transformation which hinders their response to the rapidly changing social situations. Therefore, today the Church in India has a specific task of reaching out to the people in their social situations through proclamation of liberation and social justice which is a consequence of her mission to preach the Gospel to the poor.[269]

There are some like Fr. G. Cosmon Arokiaraj, a Dalit priest and executive secretary for the CBCI office of Scheduled Castes and Backward Classes who believe that attitudes in the Church will not change until the government helps raise Dalit Christians' social standing through reservation. On the other hand, there are other Dalit Christians like Ram Bharati, an Anglican Dalit who leads the Poor Christian Liberation Movement (PCLM), who disagree with this view. They would want Indian churches to serve Dalits rather than pass the buck to the government.[270]

In such a situation the example of Ambedkar, who single-handedly faced the wrath of the Caste Hindus so as to obtain the human rights for the Untouchables, stands out as a model for us today. In this regard, his insights on 'social humanism' give an apt response to the social exigency of our times. His social philosophy stresses the need of the synthetic outlook on life, avoiding all extremes of individualism and socialism, hedonistic materialism and ascetic spiritualism. It thus, aims at securing an integrated human personality as well as emotionally integrated human society.

Ambedkar, in the final evaluation, is a thinker relevant to our times, who welcomes the spirit of humanism and demands the fundamental rights of the individual by upholding democracy and condemning dictatorship and totalitarianism. One witnesses in him the concern for the total human being. His 'social humanism' is not a close-ended synthesis but it is to be kept open to our social reality as it has emerged in response to our particular human life situation.

Ambedkar is an authentic prophet of our era, who has dared to testify to the human reality and to our forgetfulness and deliberate

---

[269] Menezes, "Response of the Indian Church to Social Issues", 282-290.

[270] Megan Sweas, "Caste First, Christ Second, for some Indian Christians" *Religion Dispatches,* July 9, 2012. http://religiondispatches.org/Caste-first-christ-second-for-some-indian-christians/ Accessed on 16/4/2018.

avoidance of it. He has offered us not a system to be applied to reality blindly. Instead, authentic to the need of our times, he has provided us with an orientation in our own social struggle. In today's world, Ambedkar is challenging…challenging us to create a humanistic vision of reality for ourselves and the others around us, and to live it in creating it.

Bibliography

Primary Sources

Books

Ambedkar, B.R. *Pakistan or the Partition of India*. Bombay: Thacker and Co. Ltd, 1946.

_______. *States and Minorities*. Bombay: Sindhu Publication Private Limited, 1947.

_______. *The Buddha and His Dhamma*. Bombay: Siddharth College Publication, 1957.

_______. *Annihilation of Caste*. Jalandhar: Bheem Patrika Publications, 1968.

_______. *Why go for Conversion*. Bangalore: Dalit Sahitya Academy, 1987.

Articles

Ambedkar, B.R. "Buddha and the future of his religion." 1950 as cited in D.R. Jatava, *The Critics of Dr. Ambedkar*. New Delhi: Bhartiya Shoshit Jan Uttan Parishad, 1975.

_______. "Buddhism and Communism." Speech at the closing session of the Fourth Conference of the World Fellowship of Buddhist in the State Gallery Hall in Kathmandu (Nepal) on 20th

November 1956. As cited in D.R. Jatava, *The Social Philosophy of B.R. Ambedkar*. Agra: Phoenix Publication House, 1965.

_______. "Castes in India." *Writings and Speeches*. Vol. 1. Bombay: The Education Department - Government of Maharashtra, (1979): 5-22.

_______. "Annihilation of Caste: With a Reply to Mahatma Gandhi." *Writings and Speeches*. Vol. 1. Bombay: The Education Department - Government of Maharashtra, (1979): 23-35.

_______. "Annihilation of Caste." The speech prepared for the 1936 Annual Conference of the Jat-Pat-todak Mandal of Lahore but not delivered owing to the cancellation of the Conference by the Reception Committee on the ground that the views expressed in the Speech would be unbearable to the Conference. *Writings and Speeches*. Vol. 1. Bombay: The Education Department - Government of Maharashtra, (1979): 36-80.

_______. "Philosophy of Hinduism." *Writings and Speeches*. Vol. 3. Bombay: The Education Department - Government of Maharashtra, (1987): 3-92.

_______. "The Woman and the Counter-Revolution." *Writings and Speeches*. Vol. 3. Bombay: The Education Department - Government of Maharashtra, (1987): 429-437.

_______. "The Condition of the Convert." *Writings and Speeches*. Vol. 5. Bombay: The Education Department - Government of Maharashtra, (1989): 445-476.

_______. "Preface." *Writings and Speeches*. Vol. 7. Bombay: The Education Department - Government of Maharashtra, (1990): 9-19.

_______. "The Riddle of the Shudras." *Writings and Speeches*. Vol. 7. Bombay: The Education Department - Government of Maharashtra, (1990): 21-36.

_______. "The Number of Varnas, Three or Four." *Writings and Speeches*. Vol. 7. Bombay: The Education Department - Government of Maharashtra, (1990): 132-139.

_______. "Brahmins *Versus* Shudras" *Writings and Speeches.* Vol. 7. Bombay: The Education Department - Government of Maharashtra, (1990): 140-155.

_______. "The Degradation of the Shudras" *Writings and Speeches.* Vol. 7. Bombay: The Education Department - Government of Maharashtra, (1990): 156-185.

_______. "Why do the Untouchables live outside the Village?" *Writings and Speeches.* Vol. 7. Bombay: The Education Department - Government of Maharashtra, (1990): 271-277.

_______. "Are the Untouchables Broken Men?" *Writings and Speeches.* Vol. 7. Bombay: The Education Department - Government of Maharashtra, (1990): 278-280.

_______. "Are there Parallel Cases?" *Writings and Speeches.* Vol. 7. Bombay: The Education Department - Government of Maharashtra, (1990): 281-283.

_______. "How did Separate Settlements for Broken Men disappear elsewhere?" *Writings and Speeches.* Vol. 7. Bombay: The Education Department - Government of Maharashtra, (1990): 284-285.

_______. "Racial Difference as the Origin of Untouchability" *Writings and Speeches.* Vol. 7. Bombay: The Education Department - Government of Maharashtra, (1990): 289-304.

_______. "Occupational Origin of Untouchability" *Writings and Speeches.* Vol. 7. Bombay: The Education Department - Government of Maharashtra, (1990): 305-307.

_______. "Contempt for Buddhists as the Root of Untouchability" *Writings and Speeches.* Vol. 7. Bombay: The Education Department - Government of Maharashtra, (1990): 311-317.

_______. "Did the Hindus never eat Beef?" *Writings and Speeches.* Vol. 7. Bombay: The Education Department - Government of Maharashtra, (1990): 323-328.

_______. "What made the Brahmins become Vegetarians?" *Writings and Speeches.* Vol. 7. Bombay: The Education Department - Government of Maharashtra, (1990): 334-349.

_______. "Why should Beef-eating make Broken Men Untouchables?" *Writings and Speeches.* Vol. 7. Bombay: The

Education Department - Government of Maharashtra, (1990): 350-355.

Secondary Sources

Azariah, M. *The Un-Christian Side of the Indian Church*. Bangalore: Dalit Sahitya Academy, 1989.

Baker, Sophie. *Caste*. Calcutta: Rupa and Co, 1991.

Benn, S.I. and Peters R.S., *Social Principles and the Democratic State*. London: Allen & Unwin, 1959. As cited in D.R. Jatava, *The Social Philosophy of B.R. Ambedkar*. Agra: Phoenix Publication House, 1965.

Ghurye, G.S. *Caste and Class in India*. Bombay: The Popular Book Depot, 1950.

Hutton, J. H. *Caste in India*. Bombay: Oxford University Press, 1963.

Jatava, D.R. *The Critics of Dr. Ambedkar*. New Delhi: Bhartiya Shoshit Jan Uttan Parishad, 1975.

_______. *The Political Philosophy of B.R. Ambedkar*. Agra: Phoenix Publication House, 1965.

_______. *The Social Philosophy of B.R. Ambedkar*. Agra: Phoenix Publication House, 1965.

Keer, Dhananjay. *Dr. Ambedkar: Life and Mission*. Bombay: Popular Prakashan, 1954.

Marx and Engels. *On Religion*. Moscow: Progress Publishers, 1957.

Articles

Dalmia, Yashodhara. "Scheduled Castes – A View from below." *The Times of India*, December 15, 1974. As cited in D.R. Jatava, *The Critics of Dr. Ambedkar*. New Delhi: Bhartiya Shoshit Jan Uttan Parishad, 1975.

Editorial. "The Bishops' Concerns." *The Examiner*, Vol. 143, January 25, 1992. 1.

Gandhi, M. K. "Dr. Ambedkar's Indictment." *Harijan*, August 15, 1936. As cited in D.R. Jatava, *The Critics of Dr. Ambedkar*. New Delhi: Bhartiya Shoshit Jan Uttan Parishad, 1975.

_______. "Dr. Ambedkar's Indictment." *Harijan*, July 18, 1936. As cited in D.R. Jatava, *The Critics of Dr. Ambedkar*. New Delhi: Bhartiya Shoshit Jan Uttan Parishad, 1975.

Menezes, Baptist. "Response of the Indian Church to Social Issues." *Indian Theological Studies*, Sept-Dec' 91, 259-279.

Prabhu, Pandharinath J. *Hindu Social Organization*. Bombay: Popualr Prakashan, 1961.

Prasad, R.A. *Socialist Thought in Modern India*. Meerut: Meenakshi Publications, 1974.

Rakshekar, V.T. "Chundur proves non-Hindu Dalit can't live with Hindus Separate electorate and settlement as solution." *Dalit Voice,* Vol. 10, September 1-15, 1991, 3-11.

_______. "Reddy's strip BC woman." *Dalit Voice,* Vol. 10, September 16-31, 1991, 11-12.

_______. "Reservations meant to elevate, empower a group but not an individual." *Dalit Voice,* Vol. 11, December 16-31, 1991, 19-21.

_______. *Merit, My Foot*. Bangalore: Dalit Sahitya Academy, 1987.

_______. *The Dilemma of Class and Caste in India*. Bangalore: Dalit Sahitya Academy, 1984.

Shouri, Father. "Dalit Christians threat to walk out of 'Hindu' Church." *Dalit Voice,* Vol. 10, August 16-31, 1991, 13-18.

Internet Articles

"Caste discrimination in India." IDSN Briefing Note – India 2016, 1-6. http://idsn.org/wp-content/uploads/2016/09/IDSN-briefing-note-India-2016.pdf Accessed on 8/4/2018.

Debnath, Bodhisattwa. "Caste Discrimination in India: 10 Cases You Wish Did Not Happen." May 19, 2016 1-10. https://blog.timetoswipe.com/Caste-discrimination-india-10-cases-you-wish-did-not-happen/ Accessed on 8/4/2018.

"Dalit Theology: A Transforming Grace for the Indian Church" https://www.scribd.com/document/300019581/Dalit-Theology Accessed on 25/4/2018.

IDSN. "Caste Discrimination" http://idsn.org/Caste-discrimination. Accessed on 8/4/2018.

Sweas, Megan. "Caste First, Christ Second, for some Indian Christians" *Religion Dispatches,* July 9, 2012. http://religiondispatches.org/Caste-first-christ-second-for-some-indian-christians/ Accessed on 16/4/2018.

"Untouchability in India" http://www.azadindia.org/social-issues/Untouchability-in-india.html Accessed on 25/4/2018.

"Untouchability in India" http://www.indiacelebrating.com/social-issues/Untouchability-in-india/ Acessed on 25/4/2018.